PRAISE FOR KEVIN LILES AND
MAKE IT HAPPEN

"Kevin Liles gives practical advice on making your career dreams a reality, just like he did . . . a great read."

—*Teen People* (from the "Hot List")

". . . a hip guide to success with poignant stories and powerful lessons that will teach all the flavors of humanity."

—Dr. Mehmet Oz, author of *YOU: The Owner's Manual*

"*Make It Happen* is a guide for all of you who want to succeed in the music industry—and in life. Kevin provides the tools he has developed from his experiences and mistakes and teaches you how to apply them to your own journey."

—Terrie Williams, author of *Stay Strong: Simple Life Lessons for Teens*

"Kevin Liles brings unique insight to business . . . and life in general. At the core of his success is a deep understanding of people and a simple, direct way of communicating with them."

—Larry Probst, chairman and CEO, Electronic Arts

"Liles offers advice on how to strategize, look ahead, embrace a hard-knock life, find a mentor and learn from failure."

—*Vibe*

"Prepare yourself for some powerful and unconventional answers to the big question of 'making it.' Liles is a perfect example of how, with the proper focus and drive, being yourself can lead to triumph and achievement."

—Cathy Hughes, chairman and founder, Radio One

"Kevin Liles has a timeless, if unexpected, message for the hip-hop generation. Beneath the bling-bling and often obscured by outsized and outrageous personalities, business success still requires vision, focus, discipline and execution. The styles may change, but the basics remain the same."

—Price M. Cobbs, M.D., author of *My American Life: From Rage to Entitlement*

Also available as an eBook

MAKE IT HAPPEN

The Hip-Hop Generation Guide to Success

KEVIN LILES

With Samantha Marshall

ATRIA BOOKS

New York   London   Toronto   Sydney

ATRIA BOOKS

1230 Avenue of the Americas
New York, NY 10020

The Library of Congress has cataloged the hardcover edition as follows:

Liles, Kevin.
  Make it happen : the hip-hop generation guide to success / Kevin Liles ; with
Samantha Marshall.
    p.   cm.
    1. Success in business—Handbooks, manuals, etc. I. Marshall, Samantha, 1966–
II. Title.

HF5386.L595 2005
650.1—dc22

2005048075

ISBN-13:   978-0-7434-9736-7
ISBN-10:   0-7434-9736-8
ISBN-13:   978-0-7434-9737-4 (Pbk)
ISBN-10:   0-7434-9737-6 (Pbk)

First Atria Books trade paperback edition September 2006

10   9   8   7   6   5   4   3   2   1

ATRIA BOOKS is a trademark of Simon & Schuster, Inc.

Manufactured in the United States of America

For information about special discounts for bulk purchases,
please contact Simon & Schuster Special Sales at
1-800-456-6798 or business@simonandschuster.com.

The author gratefully acknowledges permission from the following sources to reprint
material in their control: Arista Records for an excerpt from "The What," written and
performed by The Notorious B.I.G. and Method Man, Tee Tee, Inc./Janice Combs
Music (BMI), © 1994 Arista Records, Inc.; Def Jam Records for an excerpt from
"Mona Lisa," lyrics by Ricky Walters, performed by Slick Rick, © 1988 DEF JAM
RECORDINGS, UNIVERSAL MUSIC PUBLISHING and for an excerpt from "Jack
The Ripper," written by J.T. Smith, R. Rubin, performed by LL Cool J, coproduced by
Dwayne Simon, assistant producers: Steve Ett and Brian Latture, additional
production: Rick Rubin (ASCAP), © 1988 Def Jam Recordings, Inc. and an excerpt
from "More or Less" (J. Barrow, K. West, B. Miller, J. Bradford, F. Gorman),

Page 245 constitutes an extension of the copyright page.

This book is dedicated to the Struggle. For who we are not supposed to be and what we are not supposed to know. For the dreams we are not supposed to dream and the love for one another we are not supposed to show.

For now I understand, the bad before the good, the storm before the sunshine, the loss before the win and the down before the up. The Struggle made me stronger and for that I dedicate this book to hip hop for through you anything is possible!

ACKNOWLEDGMENTS

Foundation

I would like to thank my parents, Jerome and Alberta Fennoy, for pushing me to be more than a product of my environment; for not allowing me to settle for what made me happy for the moment; and for providing me with family values in which I base my whole existence. I am a product of you.

To my grandparents, Charles and Icelene Bowie, thank you for traveling this thirty-seven year journey with me. Your wisdom, encouragement and sense of community have given me so much solid ground to stand on. You raised me to be a leader; therefore, I lead for you. You guys are my rock.

Granddad I know you are watching. I just hope I continue to make you proud. Your spirit is with me everyday.

I would like to thank the city of Baltimore. Please allow me to be your symbol of Hope. For I have walked the same streets, learned in the same schools and breathed the same air. It is about where I'm from because it helped me get to where I am. I truly BELIEVE.

Cultivation

I would like to thank my teachers, mentors, coaches, colleagues, bosses (especially Russell Simmons and Lyor Cohen), extended family and friends. There are so many of you, yet not enough words to express my appreciation for your continued support. Thank you all for caring!

I would like to thank Atria/Simon & Schuster and Ms. Sam Marshall for believing in me and in my message. Sam, because we both have higher callings, this book is only the beginning.

Inspiration

I would like to thank my beautiful children, Kevin, Kayla and Khristen; my sisters, Teia and Tiffany Fennoy; and my brother, Aaron. We share the same blood; therefore, my river runs deep with love for each of you.

In search of my true calling, God in you I find strength, wisdom, comfort and courage.

I surrender; therefore, I am here to serve.

In memory of my grandfather

Charles Wesley Bowie

3/22/12–7/21/91

CONTENTS

INTRODUCTION:
FROM INTERN TO PRESIDENT

My cousin Tony always told me there are three kinds of people in this life: those who make it happen, those who watch it happen and those who let it happen to them. Which kind do you want to be?

From early on, I decided to take control of my fate and put myself in that first category. If I was ever going to be a success in life, I had no choice.

On the streets of West Baltimore where I'm from, you don't get handed a comfortable living. Every day is a struggle to survive. My hometown is one of the crime capitals of America. Every year, about three hundred people are murdered. As a young black man, I stood a better chance of getting shot or thrown in jail than getting a good-paying and respectable job.

I love where I'm from, but I wasn't going to let myself become another statistic. I didn't just want to survive. I wanted to be a success.

That's what hip hop is all about. Despite what you read about the bling, the Bentleys, the Benzes and the beefs, those are trappings that have nothing to do with the true spirit of the culture. We are all about overcoming the odds and making success happen for ourselves by being ourselves, only better. Whatever our detractors say, we pulled ourselves out of the ghetto the old-fashioned way—through hard work.

Every real success story in hip hop comes down to the same thing: someone who finds the will, focus and drive to achieve. It doesn't matter if you are male or female. It doesn't matter what race or religion you are. It doesn't even matter what hustle you choose.

You could be a firefighter, a rapper, a banker, an athlete or a nurse. If you fight against the odds to realize a dream and be the best that you can be at whatever industry you choose, you are doing it the hip-hop way.

We don't take no for an answer. We don't abide the negativity of people who tell us, "You can't." We'll fight to turn a "no" into a "yes." For us, impossible is nothing.

If I had let the statistics define me, I wouldn't even be here. When I was fourteen I watched another kid get beaten close to death with a baseball bat. When I was eighteen one of my homeboys was shot in the head at a basketball game over some beef.

I was no angel. I did things that were strictly dumb. My friends and I used to hustle car stereos, whatever could get us a few dollars. We'd steal stuff, just for the thrill of it. Once or twice I came inches from getting thrown in jail.

The day of my high school graduation from Woodlawn High was a turning point. So many of my buddies didn't make it. The time for playing around was over. Still in my graduation gown, gripped by a sudden panic, I stood on the street outside the commencement hall and turned to my mother.

"Ma, what am I going to do now?"

My mother, Alberta Fennoy, made all the reassuring noises good parents do, telling me I could do anything I put my mind to.

"Kevin," she said. "You will be successful, you just have to decide that you want to be."

To me, at that time, success was a secure job paying $30,000 a year. I wanted a roof over my head and the ability to provide for my family. Unlike a few of my classmates who were going on to top colleges, I didn't have a rich dad or an uncle who could bring me into their business. If they weren't on the hustle, the kids from my neighborhood were taking minimum-wage jobs flipping beef patties at some fast-food joint.

I chose a different path: business. I made it from intern to president of Def Jam in nine years, before I turned thirty. Today, at just thirty-seven, I'm executive vice president of Warner Music Group, a multibillion-dollar content company that's one of the biggest in the music industry.

My hard work has given me so much success, access and opportunity that I now experience things most of us only dream of: travelling by private planes, vacations in places I never knew existed and the best of the best that life has to offer. I've gone from what I thought was rich to creating one hundred–year estate wealth planning so my children's great-grandchildren will receive the fruits of my labor.

So how did I make it happen? As I look back over the last decade, it's a question I've been asking myself a lot lately. I know I've been blessed. Some of those kids I grew up with are still there on the corner, many struggling to survive, many more not making it, ending up in jail or worse.

But my success is no accident. I made it happen because I had the will. I didn't have the history of Russell Simmons or Lyor Cohen, who were there from the beginning and founded Def Jam. I came late to that block party. I didn't have the street credibility of a rapper from Hollis, Queens. In the business of hip hop, I was the outsider who started from next to nothing.

If I can do it, so can you. Anyone can make it happen, but they have to want it badly enough. I was strategic, hardworking, devoted to the brand and passionate about every aspect of this business, from wiping down a stage before a concert to choosing the cover of LL Cool J's next album. I didn't just find a job, I found my one true love.

It didn't always occur to me that being a businessman could be cool. I always knew I wanted to make money, but by age fifteen I was determined I was going to be a rapper. I joined a group with my friends. We had dreams of making it. Back then, we looked up to the drug dealer on the corner, the NBA stars, artists like Run DMC. Who, me, sit in an office pushing papers? Nah! To hell with that!

But take it from me as a music executive—a lot more people can make it in business than as a rapper, basketball player, boxer or in the crack game. Even the most talented singers and athletes don't always make it. Many who do get there have crashed and burned because they don't even know the basics of business.

Business is a democracy. You don't need to be born with a God-given right hook or the gift of a great voice. The business world is the only truly level playing field. Anything is possible if you work hard and show results; you *can* make it. Whoever you are, you will be measured by what you bring to the bottom line and the work ethic that you play by.

Business doesn't have to be about a bunch of guys in suits. Just look at Def Jam. You'll be hard-pressed to find an executive over forty at that label. It was never an exclusive club. It was built on not having access. We fed on talent, drive and passion, not connections, politics or pedigrees. Creating access and opportunity is the hip-hop way.

We've changed the meaning of the hustle from something that you do to people in a negative way to working harder and longer than everybody else. We might not be as smart, but we made a niche and found a way. Our culture has created a mindset that mainstream America wants to emulate.

People used to say hip hop would die. Twenty-five years later, they're still saying it, and we're more alive than ever. Our culture used to be out on the fringes, something to be dismissed. But we've survived because of the maturation of our culture and the "Browning of America." We are where it's at today. We own the youth market that corporations desperately want a piece of.

The rest of the world is latching on to hip hop to sell everything from hamburgers to mobile phones. You can't turn on the

TV without seeing ads that refer to our culture. Soda, sneakers, airlines, JCPenney back-to-school sales and even the Serta counting-sheep are rapping.

Of course, hip hop is more than just a mainstream marketing tool. It's been embraced by the masses around the world. We're part of the fabric of cultures from Africa to China to Russia to Colombia. We've become the voice of the struggle everywhere.

We couldn't have become this big without grinding hard and running ourselves like a professional organization. We had to. Back in the day, and even now, the corporate world didn't want to let us in. We had to prove ourselves and do everything better so the businesses of mainstream America would come knocking on our door.

In the words of Jay-Z, "So now you own a record label, I got one too / We on a roll now, can't nobody stop our crew."

As successful as companies like Def Jam, FUBU, Sean Jean, Rocawear and Phat Farm are, it hasn't always been easy to get a meeting. Daymond John got so tired of getting turned down by the big national clothing distributors that he struck out on his own. Now he owns the corners of major department stores across America. FUBU means: For Us, By Us. That's the hip-hop creed.

Corporate executives hear the music their kids like, listen to hip-hop haters in the media like Bill O'Reilly and they get scared. They still don't get our lyrics. They don't appreciate the positive in the message. Like Jack Nicholson's character Jessop says in the movie *A Few Good Men,* "You can't handle the truth!"

Our artists sing about doing it for themselves and coming up from a life of poverty. Sometimes the message is materialistic. They rap about Louis Vuitton and Jacob watches. They celebrate the stuff they can afford today that they couldn't even dream about when they were kids.

Sometimes our words are violent and angry. But even the

nastiest lyrics can be educational. They reflect the raw truth of the world many rap artists come from. They've earned the right to be defiant. Like Russell says, "We don't adapt to you, you adapt to us."

But that doesn't mean we are entitled to our success. To make it happen you need to get educated and learn the skills. You need to play your position to the best of your ability. Be disciplined. Be tough, especially on yourself. Find the passion to succeed and the will to learn and you can make it.

It won't be easy. Success doesn't come without a few failures, and every struggle against poverty has its fallen soldiers. We've lost some of our greatest artists—Biggie, Jam Master Jay, Tupac—to the violence that comes from jealousy, desperation and ignorance.

The traditional music business has also taken a beating. We've had a slump in the record industry because of piracy and illegal downloading. Hundreds of jobs were lost. I have personally had to lay off dozens of close friends at Def Jam. We got sued for tens of millions of dollars. It ate up even more of our profits. My mentor, Lyor Cohen, left Def Jam for Warner. I didn't know where I stood. After a tumultuous few months, I followed, but it hurt my heart to leave the label I grew up with.

It's moments in life like those that remind you that even when you think you've got it all, it can always be taken away. As soon as we start thinking we deserve our place at the top of the heap, God lets us know that what he gives he can so easily take away.

That's why the hip-hop way to success can be of value at any stage in a career. We don't give up. We turn disadvantage into advantage. We've learned to reinvent ourselves with each new business we take on. We keep the passion burning by constantly pushing and stretching ourselves. When other people knock our hustle, we get stronger.

I don't pretend to have all the answers. If I said I knew every secret to success, you'd know I was full of it. Thirty-seven may be old to some of you, but I don't have enough gray hairs to be some sage. I'm still on a steep learning curve.

I've been grinding in the trenches for so long that this is the first time in my life I've lifted my head up. I'm working hard to figure out how to bring more balance to my life. I'm making the transition from running a small entrepreneurial business hands-on, to taking a more senior executive role. I have to learn to put the right people in the right positions. I have to learn how to delegate so that I can see the big picture, have a life and stop putting out every little fire on my own.

But I can take you on the journey that got me to this point. I can tell you how I got this far, and what's going to get me through and take me further as I deal with all the changes in my world.

Through this book, you'll get to know my story. How an ordinary kid from Baltimore made it from intern to president at the company of his dreams. I'll take you back to my grandmother's small house on Presstman Street. I'll tell you about my first hustle, my biggest screwups and the toughest decisions I ever made in my life.

You'll hear how I joined a rap group, Numarx, when I was sixteen, and how, in 1986, we wrote the hit single "Girl You Know It's True," which helped the spandex pop duo Milli Vanilli lip-sync their way to a Grammy. We sued their record label for taking our song and won the royalties and our rights.

That experience taught me how artists need to know the business of music. That's when I found my mission. Instead of continuing my career as an artist, I took a job as an unpaid intern at Def Jam. I was willing to do anything to get to the heart of the hip-hop music industry.

I'll also draw on the examples of friends, mentors and executives from all industries. I'll tell you about the drive and determination of Ludacris, who made his own album when no other record label would sign him. I'll tell you about how Jay-Z refuses to be swayed until he's thought things through with his brilliant analytical mind.

I'll share my conversation with Bob Johnson, the founder and CEO of Black Entertainment Television, the biggest black-owned and -operated media empire in the world. BET became a reality because one man believed it was possible.

I'll introduce you to Walter Randolph, my twenty-three-year-old assistant, who was so determined to make it in the music business that he'd sleep on the subway and do any odd job just so that he could learn at Def Jam University.

You'll meet Russell Simmons, who understands the difference between true success and just getting paid. Over the years, Russell has taught me that it's not the stuff but the work itself that matters. Real success is happiness. It's the joy of focusing on a project or cause you truly believe in and the very act of making it happen that is its own reward.

I want you to learn from my mistakes as well as my best plays. Taking risks and facing failure are both ways to come correct. At Def Jam, we always loved the employees willing to stick their necks out and get bold with an idea, even if we shot them down. That's how we'd grow.

Like Lyor's mom told him when he was a kid, take the biggest risks when you're young. You've got less to lose when you mess up, and more often than not you can get the biggest rewards.

I didn't do it all by myself. I had family and mentors to guide me. I realized early on that the best resource is the "human resource." My family started out poor enough for me to remember the government cheese, the spam and the WIC checks. But my mother and my father, Jerome, the man she married after my birth father left us, worked hard to provide me and my brother and sisters with a comfortable home.

My parents were strict but supportive. They believed in me

and encouraged me in sports, music, Boy Scouts, football, whatever I wanted to try. I used to complain that we were "Family America." To my teenage mind, our wholesome home life was so not cool. But it was a gift that saved me.

Not everyone is as blessed with a stable home life. So many successful entrepreneurs from the culture come from broken homes. But even without these solid foundations, you have to have the drive and passion inside you to make it happen.

In the words of my mother, Alberta, "People are always going to tell you what you can't do, but if you work hard and believe in yourself, you'll prove them all wrong."

So whatever life hands you, NO MORE EXCUSES! If you don't believe my mom, heed the words of the late, great Biggie Smalls:

> F___ the world don't ask me for sh__
> 'Cause everything you earn, you gotta work hard for it.

Let this book be your companion as you make your way through your working life. Let my example, and the example of those around me, inspire you to be the best janitor, nurse's aide, business executive, ditch digger, entrepreneur, lawyer, teacher or cop you can be. Self-respect comes from any job well done. You are your own best business. You are your biggest brand.

Let my words guide you onto a new path of hope. Your future doesn't have to be a stereotype. Whether you think you have to work as a gardener or a maid because that's what your parents did. Whether you grew up in the projects and think you have to sell crack because that's what the guy on the corner does.

Whether you just lost your job on Wall Street and you think your career is over. Whether you've hit a wall and hate what you're doing but think it's too late to change fields. The only ghetto that can hold you down is the ghetto of the mind. The only thing holding you back is your state of mind. We can sometimes be our worst enemy and biggest obstacle. It's time for change.

Live by my ten rules and remember: in hip hop, we don't get down, we get UP!

Empower yourself and . . . MAKE IT HAPPEN!!!

Find Your Will

You better lose yourself in the music, the moment

You own it, you better never let it go

You only get one shot, do not lose your chance to blow

This opportunity comes once in a lifetime yo

—Eminem, "Lose Yourself"

Willpower starts deep inside you. You can't have ambition without will and the burning passion to do something. Go find your passion.

Figure out what you want, and what you're willing to sacrifice to get it. Some people call it a dream, a mission or a vocation. I call it will. Whatever word you choose, the idea is to identify something that takes you outside of yourself and helps you envision your future. Name it and claim it.

Everyone has a dream or something they love to do. Whether it's about making it big as a rapper or selling enough insurance policies to afford that dream vacation, if your will is strong enough, it will get you through the hard knocks that might otherwise throw you off the path to success.

Tapping into your will can take time. It's an imperfect

process of trial and error. Sometimes we think we know what we want because we are trying to live up to other people's expectations. Maybe you're studying accounting because your parents want you to find a steady job, but you hate working with numbers. Maybe you're working as a hairdresser because your mother made a good living at it, but weaving, crimping, cutting and straightening hair is boring you to death.

People from our culture don't always get to know what they want because they weren't exposed to the possibilities. They are only thinking they will be a product of their environment. They're too caught up in surviving in the streets, struggling on welfare, or dealing with a father or mother in prison. Kids think if they're going to escape their corners and see the world, they'd better join the army.

Their only limitation is that they don't know the game. But awareness can change that.

No Guts, No Glory

There's an underground card game we like to play while we're killing time backstage or just hanging out with our homeboys. It's called "Guts."

Guts is a street version of poker, but in this game everybody gets dealt three cards. Each player has to put $100 in the pot, so if you've got ten people playing, it's $1,000 at the start of the first round. Once you've been dealt your hand, the dealer calls his game. He can say, "One, two, three, drop." Everyone can either hold their cards up or, if they're not going to stay in, drop them. If you've got guts, if you feel you can win, you hold your cards up to see if you or the others have to match what's in the pot. Calling "guts" helps us flush out the people who aren't real players.

The stakes get high, especially when you have a sizeable crew in on the game. One night last year, for example, we had seventeen guys playing Guts at Jay-Z's Manhattan nightclub, 40/40. Jay and his partner in the club, Juan; NBA stars LeBron James and Antoine Walker and their crews; Richard Santulli, founder of the private jet company NetJets; Mike Kyser and Steve Stoute, "the Mayor" and marketing wiz of Def Jam respectively, were all in the game. I was the dealer, presiding over a pot that quickly got up to $40,000 just in that first round.

As the dealer, I get to hold my cards until the end and I'm the first person to call guts. Once you call it, all the players have to turn their cards up. The best hand wins, and the losers have to match the pot. Of the five people left in that game, Juan won.

Sometimes the pot gets so big that people are afraid to keep playing and they drop out. If everyone does that you might get to walk even if you're bluffing. Nobody shows their hand and you can put yours back in the deck without having to pay. But we never let people walk. That's why it usually costs people a minimum of $10,000 just to play one round with us.

Wherever we are on the road, me, Jay and the rest of my crew get together for a Guts game. It's become a tradition. We all come as our different characters. Jay-Z's is "Lucky Lefty," because anyone who gets stuck sitting to the left of him loses. They call me "The Cowboy," because they know Kevin Liles is going to shoot you down. I'm not going to let you walk. I'm going to call it in every game. I say, "I'm not letting any of you feel y'all are better than me, so 'Guts!' "

Do you have the guts? Do you have the courage to stay in the game all the way and risk it all? No matter what your face looks like, no matter what's happening in your career, no matter who's in your ear telling you what you should and should not do, no matter who's saying you can't, do you have the will to keep it going? To play Guts, you have to want to win more than anything. You have to overcome your fear. That's what this game is all about.

One of my former employees, Shante Bacon, always has guts. She was just a college rep for us when she first joined Def Jam. But she'd known all her young life that she was destined to work in the music business. Even as a teenager she figured one day she'd run her own label.

When Shante was in college she was a rep for Def Jam's distribution company in Virginia. That means she promoted our label, and any new singles that were coming out, through college parties, football games, homecomings, college radio and concerts. One day in her senior year she sent us a three-hundred-page book she'd put together documenting all the work she'd done for Def Jam over the years. She included wrap-ups of events, pictures and dozens of letters of congratulations from me and Lyor on the success of her work on campus. She put it together in one slick package using everything she'd learned as a marketing major. I'd never met Shante, but I took one look at that book and said, "She's hired."

That was in November 1997, but Shante didn't graduate until May 1998. We wanted her to join Def Jam so badly that we held the job, of sales assistant, open for her by filling it with temps. She already had the winning hand.

Lose Yourself

It's not always obvious at first what we're good at or what we enjoy doing. Some of the skills that can work in the business world don't fit easily into a box. They're not on your high school curriculum. You may even think that something you do is way too much fun to be anything but a hobby.

You may not realize it, but if you love to throw a party, you could be a great event planner. If you like to look fly, you could be a stylist. If you enjoy vibing with other people, you could be a publicist. Plenty of industries need these skills.

When I was fifteen it didn't really occur to me that I could be in a rap group. I was good in English class. I could write well. I was always composing rhymes in my spare time. My buddy Rod used to rap, so he'd come over and ask me to put together some rhymes with him, but it was just something I did for fun.

Then I heard Run DMC's hit song "Sucka MC" at a house party:

> Two years ago, a friend of mine / asked me to say some MC rhymes / So I said this rhyme I'm about to say / The rhyme was mecca, and it went this way . . .

I thought, "Damn, I can do this! Hell, I AM doing this." Rod was part of a rap group, Numarx, but it never occurred to him to ask me to join, and until that moment I never even thought about it. But when I heard that rhyme it all made sense. I had to do it.

True passion doesn't always hit you like a lightning bolt. Take my good friend and colleague, Julie Greenwald.

Julie always loved music, but she'd never even considered the music business as a career when she was going to college. She came from a nice, liberal Jewish family that believed in making a difference in the world. From the time she was a little girl she'd always planned to teach or work for some charity organization. The first thing she did when she graduated was sign up for a volunteer program to teach impoverished children in the Mississippi Delta. That year she became like a surrogate mother to these kids, who often had nothing to go home to.

But when her year ended, she moved to New York to be with her boyfriend. She found a job working as Lyor Cohen's assistant at Def Jam. Those two were kindred spirits. They'd spend hours together hatching brilliant and out-there ideas to promote artists. Julie discovered that she loved the business and decided to stay. She learned that by working in a company that was part of the hip-hop culture, she could find another, more lucrative way to serve the young people she cared so much about.

In taking care of Def Jam's consumers and providing a home away from home for the young artists who were signed to our label, Julie's nurturing instincts, together with a great head for marketing, would serve her well at Def Jam. Many of our artists come to us at such a young age, and are so messed up from the life in the streets they've come up from, that a strong, maternal figure is just what they need to set them straight. Julie's found her true vocation in the music industry. Today she works with me as president of Atlantic Records, a division of Warner Music Group.

Like Julie, you'll find your own will when you decide to look for it. Just ask yourself:

Am I a team player, or do I prefer to work on my own?
Am I creative, or do I like to plan and organize things?
Do I see the big picture, or do I like to execute the plan?
Do I like the camera, or am I that quiet guy getting it done
   behind the scenes?

If you're a detail-oriented perfectionist, or anal, like me, you might become a good chief of operations. If you're into team sports, you might make a good human resources manager, or even company president. If you're a natural-born hustler, you could be vice president of sales. In business, there's enough room for all kinds.

Step back and think about who you are and what makes you passionate. When you know who you are you'll find your fit.

By Any Means Necessary

Finding your will gives you the strength to endure whatever it takes to make it happen, even if it means sleeping on the floor of a friend's cockroach-infested apartment in the Bronx.

Walter Randolph, a lanky twenty-three-year-old kid from Chicago, wants my spot. He's followed my career path from intern to president in the music trade press. He knows that anything is possible because he's read up on it. But you won't believe what he's been willing to go through to realize his dream.

Growing up, Def Jam's music was the sound track to young Walter's life. Every job he ever worked through high school and college was in record stores, sampling and selling rap music. To him, Def Jam was the Mecca of the music business in the Holy Land of Hip Hop.

He was like thousands of other kids who travel across the country to try to get their foot in the door. He didn't aspire to be a rap artist himself. Instead, he wanted to be part of an environment that nurtures artists and creates great music that can change a culture.

At college in Tallahassee, Florida, an acquaintance of Walter's was a college rep for Sony. She'd been up to our offices in New York City to get some CDs and heard that Def Jam was hiring summer interns. She mentioned it to Walter, and his eyes lit up. He told his friend, "I'll sweep the floors, take out the garbage, ANYTHING, just get me in there!"

Immediately, he e-mailed the person in charge of recruiting interns, sending in his resume and letters of recommendation from former employers. He got a polite call back explaining the summer intern slots had already been filled, but to please try next year.

Instead, Walter kept in touch on a weekly basis, regularly following up with calls, e-mails and letters. Months later someone took a look at his resume and realized he had some valuable experience in music sales. In the middle of his junior year exams he got a call and was told to be there the next day.

What we didn't realize at the time was that Walter didn't live in New York. Truth be told we probably wouldn't have cared. So he did what he had to do, raiding his bank account for all his cash to buy a $600 last-minute plane ticket to fly up from Florida that same day. With no money left over for a hotel room, he spent the night in LaGuardia Airport's arrivals terminal and came into the city for his interview the next morning.

Walter's sacrifice paid off. He got the position, headed back home, packed all of his worldly possessions into his beat-up Chevy and drove back to his father's place in Chicago. He took a train to New York and started work with nothing but the clothes on his back.

When he started work at Def Jam Walter didn't even have a crib. We don't pay interns at Def Jam. Like me when I interned for Def Jam's regional office in Baltimore, armies of kids are willing to prove their stuff for free.

But Walter had it especially rough. After hours, he'd put his head down on a bench by the piers at Forty-seventh Street, where the cruise ships come in. He'd sleep all night on the subway. He didn't have enough money to buy food. Not eating properly gave him an ulcer.

Back then people used to say, "Walt, you work such long hours!" But he didn't want to leave the office because he had nowhere to go!

His first home, a piece of floor in a crack house in Far Rockaway, Queens, was raided one day while Walter was at work. Then Walter found a distant cousin with a free sofa in the Bronx, but he outstayed his welcome after a few weeks. Last I heard he was sharing a place with a friend in New Jersey.

He survived on the occasional hustle, and charm. Walter's polite demeanor and willingness to do anything to help made him a favorite of the girls in the office. They'd get him Phat Farm clothing samples so he could look cool. They'd order food in so he could get his three squares.

For a while there it looked to Walter like he'd never get paid. The music industry had had a lot of layoffs over the past couple of years. For the longest time I couldn't offer any of the interns full-time paid positions. They just didn't exist.

But even back in the heady days when everything we touched went platinum, most interns moved on before a full-time position opened up. They got tired of doing the stuff that nobody else wanted to do and eventually realized that making it in the music industry was just too much of a challenge for them.

Walter was an exception. No matter how tough it got, he never complained. He just kept coming to the office and working longer hours than Def Jam employees on the payroll. He made himself indispensable to me, and he knew it.

I gave him the demos that aspiring rap groups hand me outside the office so that he could tell me what, if anything, was good. I relied on him to be my eyes and ears.

Every day he'd put together a book of record spins and other daily numbers that I need to scan each morning. Known in the industry as the BDS—or Broadcast Data System—report, I call it my bible. Walter was one of the few people in the office who knew how to put it together just the way I like it.

Every day, he'd sit at the workstation outside my office taking in everything around him. When I dropped knowledge, he was there to catch it. He'd listen in on meetings and study the major players as they walked and talked through the halls. He was one of Def Jam University's best students.

He never asked me for a thing. He endured the hard times and positioned himself just right. So when I left Def Jam last year for Warner Music Group, I took him with me. Now he's getting paid.

I've got big plans for Walter.

Be Resilient

It takes tenacity like Walter's to find your passion and chase it. You have to harness your will to take success to the highest level. You have to be focused.

The dictionary says the meaning of fierce is savage or cruel. But there's more than one definition for the word. Being fierce can also mean intense, untamed, passionate and strong. The most serious are committed to going after what truly matters to them. When you are fierce, you are unstoppable.

Irv "Gotti" Lorenzo is resilient. He knew what he wanted to do before he was old enough to drive.

The head of The Inc., the multimillion-dollar record label that discovered and produced DMX, Ja Rule and Ashanti, Irv was deejaying in the community halls around Hollis, Queens, from the time he was just fifteen years old. He was so set on starting his career producing hit records and promoting talent that nothing could keep him in class. He aced every test, but his high school teachers had to flunk him because he never showed up!

But Irv didn't care. He'd already found his one true love— music.

Irv's passion is writing and producing music. But he's also down with grooming and breaking artists, and taking care of all the little details that are involved with making records and achieving bulk status in sales. He fights so hard for the artists he believes in that I call him the Muhammad Ali of the music business.

"My artist is the best and I'm going to show you guys; we

gonna sell bulk!" he announced at one of our first meetings. I had to laugh at Irv's chest-thumping style. But I was also impressed.

Irv started seeing himself as a label executive by the time he was a teenager, when Eazy-E launched Ruthless Records. He saw what Russell Simmons was doing. He watched as young dudes not much older than himself were launching labels like Bad Boy and Death Row. That's what he wanted.

Irv will stay up all night for days in a row when he's laying tracks in the studio. But as far as he's concerned, he's never worked a day in his life. Making records is pure passion. He's been involved in some huge hits, and he'll do it again and again as long as he lives and breathes.

"It all starts with the love," he said. "I would do this for free."

Irv's will was obvious from the first moment I met him. I could see in his eyes an unshakable belief in himself. He was brash but never failed to deliver. Whatever you may have heard about Irv—the FBI investigations into links with drug gangs, the recent arrests—spend five seconds with him and you know he's all about the music. He is a true record guy.

When he was just twenty-three and working for Def Jam's A&R division (artists and repertoire, for those of you not familiar with the music business), we were paying him $40,000 a year. But Irv had signed artists that grossed us $100 million in record sales. By the time he decided to branch out on his own he had our utmost respect and support.

Plenty of wannabes like to say they own a record label but most of the time it's just hype. Today, Irv is one of a rare breed of hip-hop entrepreneurs, alongside P. Diddy and Dr. Dre. He's sustained consistent success in a volatile industry where you're only as good as your last hit record.

Irv is just thirty-five, but I see him as someone who could easily take over a record label like Def Jam. That kind of success has been possible at such an early age because he dared to dream big. He's one of hip hop's great visionaries.

Quincy Jones once said, "Take the biggest dream, the biggest one you can find, and if you get just 25 percent of it, you've made it."

Take that dream and blow it up even bigger.

Repeat after me: "I believe in myself, therefore I am what I believe myself to be."

Try Everything

Don't be discouraged if you haven't found your will yet. Not everyone is like Irv. Not everyone is lucky enough to find their life's passion by the time they hit puberty. Sometimes we get stuck on the wrong path. I took many paths, just so that I could keep my options open.

It's okay to experiment. Take as many risks as you can while you're young. You wouldn't buy a car without test-driving it first, so why not try a few different things before you figure out what's going to be your life's work? Explore!

Lyor Cohen, one of the most powerful executives in the music business, calls it dabbling, and look where it's got him. Today, he's the CEO of Warner Music Group. Dick Parsons, CEO of Time Warner, was a lawyer, a political consultant and a banker before he became one of the few African-Americans to head up a Fortune 500 company. Kenneth Chenault, the CEO of American Express, started out in dental school!

Sean "P. Diddy" Combs expanded his business and widened his appeal to audiences outside of the hip-hop culture by acting in movies and playing Walter Lee in *Raisin in the Sun* on Broadway. He's got a clothing empire alongside his music empire and the sky is the limit as to what that B-boy will do next.

Trying new things always carries the risk of failure. Puffy

could have gotten his ass kicked by critics for his Broadway debut and quit. Not only did he keep it moving, he invested in his own play. He got mixed reviews and a lot of nods for making the effort to stretch himself. He brought young urban audiences into the theater for the first time and exposed them to great American drama. He puts himself out there. As Lyor would say, he leaves a piece of himself on the field every game. That alone deserves respect.

Not everything you do is going to work out, but you'll learn what works, what doesn't, what you're great at, and what you suck at. You may learn that something you love doing will be a hobby, not a career. Doing it may lead to something related that you never even thought about turning into a career.

It took me a while to figure out my true calling. My parents made sacrifices so that I would have the chance to try out all the things that captured my interest. They also pushed me to do things they knew would help me build the skills and character I would need to become a leader. They just had one condition: whatever I tried, I had to put my heart into it and see where it would take me.

I was into everything: Little League baseball, football, basketball, the Boy Scouts, the church choir. And those were just the extracurricular activities my mother knew about.

While I was earning every merit badge in the Scouts I was also hanging out with my homeboys. We'd come together on the corner of Liberty Heights and Gwynn Oaks, a rough patch of West Baltimore where we'd network with the other crews and see how much fun we could have. We were always coming up with creative ways to get the money to finance our latest needs, not all of them strictly legit.

One thing I did know early on was that I loved the power of the Almighty Dollar. I had needs. I wanted the latest sweatsuits or those Air Force Ones I'd seen at the mall. When I was eleven

I took on a paper route so that I could buy myself the nice extras my father wasn't willing to pay for. But I soon figured out that there were easier ways to earn a dollar than getting up at four in the morning every Sunday.

I graduated to shoveling snow with one of my buddies. We figured out where the old ladies lived and cleared the paths from their front doors so they wouldn't slip and fall. We clocked when a potential client would open his garage door to drive to work, so we could clear the driveway just in time. We earned hundreds of dollars in extra tips from the appreciative snow-bound masses of Baltimore!

Later on, other sources of income came from hustling. By our mid-teens, our crew had all kinds of deals going on, selling any illicit commodity we could steal or turn over for a profit. I wouldn't recommend that way of living to anyone, for reasons I'll discuss in a later chapter. But those experiences were not only lucrative, they gave me a taste for negotiating a deal and thinking fast on my feet.

I was also rapping. I wrote most of the lyrics for Numarx, including a hit song. But I was better at promoting and selling our group. I watched where the money was going. I set up our gigs. I got our music played on the radio. I planned our image and how we would invest in ourselves.

I had so many business ideas that the other guys in Numarx started calling me KG for "Krhyme Genius." One of those ideas was to start our own production company. We used our income from performing and loans from our parents, to invest in equipment for our production company, Marx Bros. Records.

My new hustle led to all kinds of interesting and profitable sidelines: street team marketing, throwing parties and promoting records on local radio. I knew every club owner, music retailer, deejay, cop and drug dealer in the mid-Atlantic who could help me push and sell records.

The sidelines continued on through high school and college. I played football at Woodlawn High for three years. By the age of nineteen I was studying to get my degree in electrical engineering and managing a telemarketing team of four hundred people for a travel marketing company called World Connections Travel.

Something had to give. The first thing to go was football. That killed me. I was one of the top high-school players in the state of Maryland, and I'd been playing football since I joined the Pop Warner league at the age of nine. I hated letting down my team.

Two years later I ditched college. I was so obsessed with music that I couldn't sit down and focus on complicated physics formulas. I'd sit in front of the computer at home and compose rhymes in my head.

Finally, my will to be in the music business was coming into focus. The hardest part was letting down my parents. My mother, Miss Berta, was disappointed. I was always close to my parents and I still am, but my decision to drop out was a turning point in our relationship. Still sore from the time I quit Boy Scouts before graduating to Eagle Scouts, they said, "Kevin, why can't you finish anything? Don't be a quitter!" But when you find your will, nothing, not even the sadness of letting down family, can stop you from going your own way.

I wasn't fully aware of it at the time, but everything I had going on from the very first dollar I earned was in some way preparing me for my career at Def Jam.

Team sports taught me the discipline needed to be a manager and work toward the good of the company. Shoveling snow and delivering newspapers taught me how to think about what the customer wants. Hustling taught me how to handle tense situations and think on my feet. Managing a telemarketing team showed me how to be a leader.

My experience with Numarx made it all clear. I wrote a song that would become one of the biggest singles in 1989, "Girl You Know It's True." National labels were clamoring to sign us to re-record it and fan the flames, but we were tied to a contract with Studio Records, a regional record label in Oxen Hill, Maryland. That didn't stop Chrysalis Records from taking it and recording it anyway as a song by Milli Vanilli.

Watching Milli Vanilli's cheesy video and hearing about those crazy record sales was galling. Our manager found us a lawyer, we sued and we won. We got the BMI award for Song of the Year, and all the royalties. At nineteen I got my first royalty check for $90,000.

At twenty, I was already bringing in $90,000 a year from my marketing job, band royalties and all my other little hustles. That was more than I could expect to make from sticking to college and graduating, so there wasn't much my mom could say.

Through all this I discovered that what I really loved was the business of music. I realized that the industry needed good music executives to take care of their own. I was twenty when I knew, more than anything, that I wanted to be part of an organization that takes care of its artists. I'd finally found my one true vocation.

Stand Up

When you find out what you want to do, stick to it. Like my football coach always said, put your head down and keep those legs moving. Your future employer will appreciate your persistence. It's no good having will unless you're willing to prove it.

Almost every employee at Def Jam who came up through the ranks—which at one time accounted for about 80 percent of the label's executives—will tell you they got their foot in the door the same way. They were beyond tenacious. You might even say they were obsessive.

By persistence, I don't just mean they sent in their resumes and followed up with a few e-mails. They came close to turning themselves into stalkers. They were shameless about using whatever contacts they had. They invented pretexts to come to the Def Jam offices. They called and called and called.

You've got to use that will you've just found to push until you've knocked down that door. There's no doorman with white gloves on waiting to open that door for you. You can't just walk right in, no matter how perfect you think you might be for the job.

I first met Deidre Graham, Def Jam's former senior vice president of marketing, when she was just twenty-two and living in L.A. Deidre's roommate Tina Davis, who was Def Jam's manager for the West Coast office back then, brought this tall, skinny kid fresh out of college to a video shoot.

Deidre had been working for some entertainment lawyer's office for about five minutes and decided that she wanted to get into "a gig that's more creative and hands-on." She asked me if I could help her and I told her I'd see what's up.

I don't think I said more than a few words to Deidre at the time, but I was impressed enough that she found a way to get my ear. There was something in the way she carried herself upright. I could tell she had that confidence and drive. No sh__! She called me for four months straight after that.

Deidre never had an actual phone conversation with me, but she called me every single day. I'd tell her to call me on Saturday morning at seven, my time, and she'd get up that morning at four L.A. time to make the call. She'd call me on my cell and I'd say call me back at three. She'd call my office and my assistant would say I was on the other line or take a message. For weeks on end she never heard my voice.

But I knew she was calling. Finally on the day of the Million Man March, I did call her back. I said, "Yo, you got the job, pick up your keys tomorrow and don't f___ up."

Deidre knew how to be just pushy enough without looking crazy to me. That's a valuable asset in any business. Like a lot of prospective employers, I like to test job candidates to see how badly they want the job.

I'm also a little indecisive about who I hire. I might meet them once and like their spirit, but I want to see if they've got what it takes. In this business, if they don't call consistently, and follow up at the precise time I tell them to, it's a bad sign because they may try even less hard once they're in. Too many kids think they're entitled.

You've got to be able to follow through and deliver, even before I put you on the payroll.

Be Shameless

I respect people who use cunning and guile to get what they want, within reason. It means their will is so strong that they've really gone to the trouble to think about how to create opportunities for themselves.

Gabrielle Peluso showed that kind of chutzpa when she got her start. She already had Def Jam in mind when she was studying communications and the music industry at Syracuse University. She was determined to get her foot in the door of the one record label she loved.

After graduation she called the New York office to see if she could get a summer internship. The person filling in for the receptionist that day said, "Oh sure, come in Monday at ten." She was kidding. But Gabby was dead serious.

She packed up her dreams in her little Volkswagen Fox and drove. The regular receptionist Sonya, who was on duty that day, was surprised to see her. When she told her she had an appointment with Jeff Trotter, the head of A&R, Sonya told her he'd left for L.A. four days earlier and wouldn't be back until Wednesday.

Suddenly it dawned on Gabby that she'd been played. She was on the verge of tears. Then she heard the receptionist tell Julie Greenwald, who was vice president of promotions at the time, that her food was in reception. She knew Julie's sister from college, but she'd never met Julie. So she pretended that she had when Julie walked through the door.

"Julie?" she said. "I'm Sina's friend, remember? We met at commencement?"

Julie didn't remember any such thing, but she was too polite to admit she had no idea who the hell Gabby was. At that point Gabby was visibly upset and the tears were flowing. She told Julie what happened. By pure coincidence the new director of video promotions needed an intern, and Julie gave her the spot. Gabby started the next day, and she's been in the building ever since.

Gabby knew that the only way she was going to get her foot in the door would be to create that opportunity for herself. If you don't know anyone, pretend that you do. Get yourself to the right parties, clubs, offices, events, and network like crazy.

Don't let fear hold you back. Your future bosses will respect you for being gutsy enough to find a way. They'll know that you'll use that same determination to get the job done. Today, Gabby is vice president of video promotions at Def Jam. She's one of the label's most valued employees.

That doesn't mean you should act crazy. Don't turn into a stalker. Deidre's persistent calls were at my invitation. Gabby walked in the door of Def Jam that day because Julie opened it for her. But as a busy executive there's nothing I hate more than being bugged by someone who's got nothing to say but can you give me a job.

A few years ago, this one guy just kept calling. I had my calls screened, because I refuse to take cold calls, so my assistant had to deal with him. Every day, several times a day, that pest would call. This guy just wouldn't give up! He begged my assistant to set up a meeting and promised her that if she did that one favor for him, he'd never bug her again. So, just to get him off her back, she did.

At eight the next morning, there he was, sitting inside my office. I entertained the guy's pitch for a few torturous minutes and sent him on his way. But my happy morning mood was ruined and I was ready to kill someone for wasting my time. He was selling a CD distribution system that I already knew was wrong for us. Otherwise, I would have called him!

There's a time and a place for everything. Not everyone is going to share your sense of urgency. Make your own luck and open up that window of opportunity, but don't piss people off!

Keep the Faith

Once you've found your will, keeping it is the hard part. It can take years for that first taste of success to come. Most people give up before it happens.

You have to love yourself enough to keep the faith. You have to believe in what you're doing even when it seems like nobody else does. If you don't, you won't be able to handle the hard knocks that I guarantee will come your way time and time again.

Russell Simmons, the godfather of hip hop and the founder of Def Jam, has achieved a level of wealth, lifestyle, social status and fame that, back in the day, no one would have thought possible for a black kid from Hollis. He's in television ads for Panasonic's newest digital delights. The culture he created is being used to sell everything from mobile phones to Mickey D's.

But over and over and over again, people used to laugh in his face. He was trying to bring hip hop, the music of the culture he loved, to the public through radio play, concerts and parties long before anyone accepted it as a legitimate form of music or business—let alone as a means to build a commercial empire.

Imagine trying to sell African-American music like the blues to middle-class white audiences before Elvis came along. Now picture trying to promote hip-hop artists long before even most black audiences found the taste for this unique combination of hard-core poetry and gritty sound.

Deejays couldn't comprehend how the rhythmic scratching of records mixed with rhymes could ever be so popular. They'd make public pleas on the radio for more music, less rap. Every time Russell held a sold-out event, people dismissed it as a fluke.

Time and again, Russell was ripped off by other promoters. All the black music industry gatekeepers figured they could afford to screw Russell and his artists. Way back when, in the late '70s, Russell gave a booker at a popular R&B club $1,900 to promote a show. The booker kept it and disappeared.

But one small event got him through and reminded him what he was striving for.

He had to escort the rap artist Kurtis Blow to Amsterdam in 1980 to perform hip hop's first hit record, "Christmas Rappin'." Russell was twenty-three years old at the time. Apart from a short hop to Philadelphia, he'd never been on a plane. Going overseas was huge! Flying first-class on KLM airlines was beyond imagination!

When he boarded the plane, the flight attendant said, "Hello Mr. Simmons, welcome aboard." He was so surprised he had to look around to see who the hell she was talking to before he clocked it was him. "From then on it was Mr. Simmons this, Mr. Simmons that, all the way to Amsterdam," Russell said. No one had ever called him Mister before.

When he deplaned, his hosts took him straight to one of those cafes where you can smoke weed. "Here we were," Russell said. "Me and Kurtis, two kids from City College in New York being given the respect and invited to smoke all the weed we wanted, legally. I was so happy!"

It may not have seemed like a big deal to anyone else. But that one gesture of respect helped bolster Russell's self-confidence and give him faith. It was a little way of saying "hey, you're important," that helped him get through the hard times and reminded him that it was all worth it.

"The thing about success is, you always have to put in more hours than you planned," he told me years later. "It happens on God's schedule, not yours. So sometimes, even though you really believe in what you're doing, you just need something to give you that little extra boost and remind you that there's dignity in the effort and it's all gonna be worth it some day."

It's these small rewards that add up to give it all meaning. They show us we're on the right path and, when the big wins come, they remind us not to take those achievements for granted. They help us keep our will in focus.

Some people don't notice or appreciate these small breakthroughs, whether it's at the beginning of their career or when they're already full-blown into it. That's a damn shame. Houses are built one brick at a time. It's these moments of achievement and nods of recognition that, when you put them together, build true success.

RULE 1

What: Find Your Will

Why: Because you need that passion to drive you to

make it happen against seemingly impossible odds.

How: Look deep within yourself to discover that thing you really love to do. It's never too late, but it's best to start young and explore everything that interests you.

But: Don't give up too early. You have to keep trying. It might not be obvious at first. We're not all born knowing we want to be doctors, lawyers or CEOs. Seek and you will find!

Do You

I maintain that nurture rather than nature is the primary molder of personality.

—Nelson Mandela

By now you've figured out what you want and found the will to make it happen. It's time to let the world know.

Your drive and determination has either brought you onto the ground floor of an organization, launched you on the entrepreneurial path or put you at the starting block of a professional career. But you still have to stand out and make it your own. You've got to brand yourself in a way that's a complement to the team. You've got to capture the market and make it your own. The next step is to find out how to Do You.

Ideally, that process would have started from the time you could walk, talk and tie your own shoelaces. The day that you are able to write your own name, the day that you are able to speak or understand what it is to put on clothes, whether it's at five or six years old, is the first opportunity that you have to handle your business. That's because the biggest business we have is ourselves.

For me, "Kevin Liles" is my most important brand. I am a reflection of my own work. If I dress like a bum, people are going to say, "That's raggedy Kev." If I don't wash up, they'll call me "dirty Kev."

Hip-hop culture has taken such hold in part because our artists are so good at branding themselves. Everyone knows that LL Cool J is the kid with the Kangol hats and one pants leg rolled up. Slick Rick the Ruler was his own unique creation. He invented "ghetto fabulous." People remember him as much for his ropes of gold and diamond-encrusted everything as for his music. Even his eye patch sparkled.

Run DMC were pioneers of branding themselves the hip-hop way. Back then, everyone else was trying to look like Rick James with the platform shoes and funkadelic clothes. Run DMC didn't care. They developed their own urban street style. They launched a whole trend with their leather suits and porkpie hats. They didn't have curls, waves or peezy hair, and they still got paid.

There was a lot of pressure back then to conform to what all the other record labels were doing and manufacture glitzy disco packaging for our artists, but letting some executive dictate how we looked wasn't true to our culture. So we did one better. We did ourselves.

At Def Jam, our philosophy was to sign stars. We wanted people with their identities fully formed. We didn't want to be the Pygmalions of hip hop, molding and shaping young no-names into our vision of what they should be.

Even if we got a lesser cut because they'd already been signed by partner labels like The Inc. or Roc-A-Fella, we'd mess with them. That's because we knew they'd been out there grinding and they could handle themselves. So did the consumer.

P. Diddy raised the bar for self-styling. Long before he started Bad Boy Records, he interned for Andre Harrell at Uptown Records. He wasn't an artist. None of us were sure exactly what he could do. But he was himself. He brought his own flava to Uptown.

Even back then, as a kid from nowhere, he was "Puff Daddy." Young Sean walked into that place with a well-formed identity. When you met him you knew he was headed for success. He wouldn't accept less than the best. It was all there in his confidence and attitude. You knew he had to go on and do his own thing because his identity and sense of himself was too strong to be part of somebody else's organization.

You don't have to be a rap artist to brand yourself. Donald Trump does Donald Trump to perfection. Some would call it extreme self-promotion and say it's a negative thing. But "the Donald" understands the hip-hop way of celebrating his own identity. He makes his swagger work for him in the business arena. Without that, he would just be another real estate developer. But now people can just look at a snapshot of the top of that man's head and know it's "Trump—real estate—Manhattan."

He is so in-your-face about his wealth, but it's calculated for an effect that's all about marketing. He embodies that lifestyle to sell it in the form of a golf club membership or a penthouse apartment overlooking Central Park. Love him or hate him, Trump has raised himself up to icon status through his reality show, "The Apprentice," his books, his endless appearances on television. He's guaranteed himself access and longevity in business because of who he is, even if his stock tanks and his casinos face foreclosure.

I'm not saying we should all be Donald Trump or P. Diddy. That's not me. That's not most people. There are subtler forms of self-branding based on the substance of what you bring to the table. But whatever your own particular flava is, figure it out now.

If you're out there, you are projecting something, period. I don't care how much you think you blend in, you are going to have some attribute that people's minds latch on to. So if the outside world is going to have an impression of who you are either way, why not take control?

You have to define your space, what you want to do and who you are, and if you are the best you can be at that, someone will want to hire you or others will want to follow you.

It's up to you to nurture your personality. You make the decision about how you are going to be seen, before somebody else shoves you into a box you don't like.

The KKK

My first experience of the power of the personal brand started early on and by accident.

When I started at Pikesville Middle School in Baltimore, the school board rezoned our district. All of a sudden, about 200 black kids descended on a school of about 800 white kids. We all had to adjust. This little experiment in integration brought all the usual tensions and baggage with it.

A couple of fights broke out. Once there was a standoff in the lunchroom over a racial slur. One of the white boys said black kids shouldn't date white kids and that the races should stick to their own kind. Another time there was a playground showdown between the races planned for after school. I don't know what would have happened. Luckily the principal found out and it was called off before anyone did anything they might regret for the rest of their life.

But I was cool. I was friendly with everybody. Me and my friends Kevin Morton and Kenny Falcon, two other black kids from elementary school, formed a clique. We called ourselves the "KKK," short for Kevin, Kenny and Kevin.

I doubt the teachers knew, although all the kids, black or white, were in on the joke. Just by being ourselves—three wiseass kids—we turned the situation at the school around with our own off-color brand of humor. It wasn't our conscious intention to break the tension, it just seemed natural to us to form an identity for ourselves in this un-PC way. We thought it was pretty funny and most of the other twelve- and thirteen-year-olds at Pikesville thought so too.

We became the cool kids. We were the go-to crew who could get anything a preteen's heart desired. We started loaning lunch money and charging interest. It happened one day when a kid came up short a dollar in the school canteen. It just popped into my head to say, "You can have a dollar but I'm gonna charge you an extra 10 percent."

I think it was all those mafia movies we grew up watching. At that time we were into *The Godfather* and *Scarface*. We were trying to be the Don Corleones of Pikesville. No one got beat up, but we were turning into three little hustlers. Soon we were getting invited to every bar mitzvah and pool party. We were the guys everyone wanted to know!

Having that special identity gave us unique access and insight into the lives of kids we wouldn't usually encounter on our corner.

Eventually we got to know a rich Jewish kid in our school called Adam. If our school bus got to the school yard too early, Adam would invite the KKK to sit and watch cartoons in the back of his dad's limousine. I couldn't believe it. Cartoons in a car! That gave me a glimpse into the kind of life I wanted to have for myself some day.

I also became friendly with the poor white kids. I used to hang out in this one boy's basement and he'd teach me to play the guitar. He was teaching me all the music from white rock bands like Motley Crü, Van Halen and Rush. That exposure opened my mind to other types of music.

Stand Out

As you make those early attempts to distinguish yourself, start with the basics.

Every day there are clusters of kids waiting outside Def Jam's headquarters at Worldwide Plaza in midtown Manhattan. The smart ones clocked that Kevin Liles was the dude who rolled up in front of the back entrance in a black Mercedes S500 every morning at eight-thirty. They'd stand and wait by the door to be ready for an opportunity to personally hand me their demo discs.

If there was some sort of manager or older guy chaperoning them, he'd tell them to dress in the same T-shirts. Lemon yellow, pastel pink, whatever they happened to find on the dollar-store racks that was the right size. They got their uniforms that identified them as a budding rap group. Visually, they succeeded in catching my attention.

I'll always accept a demo tape from any kid who has the ambition to walk up to me and hand me one. I've been there and I respect that they are trying to do something. I'll give it to my assistant, Walter, to listen to it first. If he likes it, he passes it onto me.

It's usually not the case, but on that rare occasion the demo tape is any good, I'll have a stronger impression of the kids who go the extra mile to be different from what they wore to the CD cases they handed me. There is brand power in being different. They've understood how to brand themselves at that most basic level.

One of my early lessons in the power of branding yourself came from Leon "Tuffy" Parker, my homeboy from back in Baltimore.

Tuffy used to do all kinds of stupid stuff. He was always the one in our crew who was getting into trouble. Whenever we had a hustle, he'd always take it furthest. It still amazes me, the stuff he got away with.

In his spare time, which was most of the time, Tuffy was a graffiti artist. Back in the '80s, he'd developed an aerosol signature that became instantly recognizable throughout the city. Every major building, every bus stop, every storefront, there it was, "Tuffy," written in bold black letters with a dollar sign for an extra flourish.

Soon he had a following. People were imitating Tuffy's unique signature across the city. It used to drive him crazy. He was dying to point out the fraudulent taggers, but of course, since he was defacing public property, he had to keep his mouth shut.

The Tuffy tag captured the imagination of people all over Baltimore. They wanted to know, "Who is this Tuffy?" The intrigue got so crazy that the local news channels were running stories about Tuffy the graffiti artist. The police were also interested.

Eventually, the cops caught up with him. It's the one time in his life Tuffy got arrested, and we had to bail him out. But his graffiti came to define Baltimore in the '80s. Thousands of people who lived in Baltimore at that time remember the name "Tuffy." His signature has become a permanent part of Baltimorean folklore.

To this day, Tuffy can't tell you why he did what he did. It was pretty bad when you consider that the end result was a night in jail and a lot of annoyed property owners!

But I still admire him for it. Back then, graffiti was one of the few means our culture had for public self-expression. It's not like we had access. We couldn't put out a press release to advertise our presence. We used the only outlets we had to stand up and be counted—the streets and the walls around us.

Tuffy was acting on an innate desire to make his mark in the world. It was his visual shout out to the people of Baltimore that said, "I am here, acknowledge me." He understood the fundamental truth that to exist is to express yourself and be known to the world, even if that world is just a handful of people.

Building yourself as your own brand goes much deeper than a pink shirt or a can of spray paint. We have the opportunity at an early age to form an identity that is going to make the world sit up and notice. Young or old, your own brand does matter. Don't be too late and start working on someone else's brand before you've had a chance to work on your own.

You may have already hit thirty and think you don't stand out in any particular way. You may believe that you're just average. You may feel invisible. But no one is average. You are you. You just haven't learned to accentuate what's already natural and innate to you. You have to cultivate the seeds of what is already there. Do You.

So Fresh and So Clean

It doesn't matter how much money you have, or what you think your own particular style is. There is a right way to present yourself and cultivate your own personal brand that never varies.

Like they used to say, *always* be fresh to death.

People outside the industry are surprised when they meet me. I don't fit the stereotype. I'm not flossy. I don't wear anything that sparkles. I might wear a nice watch, but that's it. While I respect the artists of this world who can carry it off, it's just not me. Hell, I don't even like the term "bling-bling." You will *never* see a half-million-dollar platinum and diamond chain in the shape of anything around my neck. I'd rather put those dollars into a house or mutual funds.

But I know how to look successful in other, below-the-radar ways that have little to do with how much money I spend. It's called good grooming.

I admit it. I get manicures. I keep my nails clean and my cuticles conditioned with cuticle oil. I keep my hair short and trimmed to the same eighth-of-an-inch length at all times. Chrisso, my barber, comes to me at the office every week. If I'm traveling, I have a regular barber in Miami or L.A. or Chicago or Atlanta, who comes to me wherever I am staying. I'm not some metrosexual. I'm just a self-respecting African-American man. I take pride in my appearance to the very last detail.

My white T-shirts are spotless. I throw them out before they have a chance to get grimy. Same with my Nike white-on-whites. I've always worn them the same way, with laces in every other hole. They have to shine. If I've worn them more than twice, I buy a new pair. I give the old ones to my father, who gives the pairs he doesn't need to charity.

My shirts are crisp. People in the office laugh at me because I iron them myself. No one else can do it right. My style may be casual and street. I wear the jeans, the Phat Farm sweats, the sneakers, the XXL-sized shirts, the Timberlands. But I am also impeccable. I would never go to an outside meeting looking sloppy. What would that say about me and my culture?

I can hear people thinking, "Well, you go through hundreds of pairs of white-on-whites at $80 each, that's a rich man's extravagance." Yes, but I earned it. I wear a lot of nice new stuff. But I've had this same look since I was a kid.

Remember when you were little and you got dressed up for church, and you got all the compliments from the grown-ups? I loved that! Now I dress neat and clean because it helps me get into the state of mind I have to be in to accomplish what I want to accomplish that day. It helps me to switch on.

When I was twelve I'd go without lunch money and take on a paper route because I wanted a new pair of tennis shoes. Me and my crew were always about looking fly.

Being fresh to death is also about attitude. Standing straight and walking tall is free. Men and women can show polish through personal refinement, no matter how much money is in their bank account.

My mother grew up poor, but she was always so well spoken and ladylike that people just assumed she was rich. I always teach my male interns to open doors for a lady. Even my seven-year-old son, Kevin Jr., knows it's always "girls first."

Making eye contact and saying please and thank you are basic rules of being civilized. But they are such rare qualities these days that showing refinement is an obvious way to make yourself stand out.

Fonzworth Bentley knew this when he invented himself. He branded himself all the way to a presenter's spot on *Access Hollywood*! Acting like the quintessential English butler was a stroke of ingenious marketing in an industry where so many artists present themselves with gangsta attitude and politeness isn't part of their posture.

But you don't have to become a caricature of class like Fonzworth. You don't have to carry a parasol to keep the sun off P. Diddy's head.

Just BE PROFESSIONAL!

Be mindful of everything you are doing. Focus your attention on the person you are with and think about how they are feeling. Answer the phone in a way you would like somebody to answer the phone when you are calling. There is an epidemic of lousy phone manners in the corporate world. You can cure that. When I answer the phone I say, "Good morning, this is Kevin Liles, how may I help you." *Not*, "Yeah."

Make sure when you give someone a report that you've checked the damn spelling. Make sure that when you say you're going to do something by a certain deadline, you deliver. When you have a meeting, think beforehand about what you want to say, and get to the point fast. Make eye contact, but don't eyeball! You want to make a connection with the person you are speaking to, not bore a hole through their eye sockets.

Just remember that class and polish are in all of us. Find it within yourself and make it a part of your everyday life. It's about showing respect for others as well as yourself. Let fine manners and professionalism be part of the brand that you project onto the world. It won't cost a thing and you'll always be remembered.

Respect Yourself

Finding your authentic self is a critical step to success. So many people don't know who they are or what they want and go into work just to get a paycheck. They go through their lives feeling like drones from nine to five. They don't identify with what they do. They disconnect from everyone and everything they deal with day to day.

You can fix that by taking ownership, even if you haven't found your dream job yet.

Say to yourself, I may be a ditch digger, but my ditches are going to be better than anybody else's. I am going to be the president of Kevin Liles' East Coast Ditch Digging. Go into it as if it is your own company. You're not just digging a ditch, you are digging your ditches, the ditches that make up the core business of the company that bears your name.

Whether it's typing a memo or greeting somebody, be accountable and responsible for that first impression. I don't want people to say that I dig bad ditches or misspell words in memos.

It's about self-respect and pride. I make sure my memos are the best memos and communicate the best message because that is how I want to be perceived, and that is how I see myself.

Branding yourself is about being self-aware, not self-conscious. To Do You is to know how to tap your soul. To Do You is to understand what things bring you happiness and a sense of balance. To Do You is to be able to react when a particular situation goes against the grain and makes you feel uncomfortable. To Do You is to be able to go into a job being the best you can possibly be.

Roger Abrahams, a philosopher and scholar of African-American culture, puts it this way: "Soul is sass because sass is one of those actions which emphasizes be-ing."

You give off a positive energy when you let your soul shine. When you aren't faking it, you're in tune with your instincts, and you can react to the moment in a way that is real. That's what hip hop has done. It represents a soul that's so powerful that it turns "no" into "yes" and opens the door for gut reaction and truth—or what Roger calls "sass."

When I interview job candidates, that's what I look for. Lauren Wirtzer, one of my first assistants, seemed qualified enough when she first came to my office on Varick Street for an interview, but I wasn't sure how much she wanted to work with us. Later that night she saw me at a party. She could have shied away and hung out with the people she already knew and felt more comfortable with, but instead she came right up to me and asked me how I was doing. She had so much energy and determination. That's what got her the job. Today she's vice president of marketing at Def Jam Enterprises, a company I started with Russell and Lyor that expands on the Def Jam brand with products like video games and mobile technology.

When I had to replace Deidre Graham as promotions manager on the West Coast, I interviewed dozens of people, but no one stood out to me. They were all kids eager for a break in the music industry but unwilling to do anything exceptional to get it. By the end of that day I was bored, and didn't expect anyone to surprise me. Then Danielle Smith walked in. Like all my interviews, it lasted about five minutes, because I don't have time for lengthy chitchat.

"Is there anything you would like to know?" I asked her on her way out.

"Yes," she said. "Can you tell me a reason why you wouldn't hire me?"

I couldn't think of one. She stumped the band! I was so bowled over by the way Danielle cut to the chase that I hired her on the spot.

Both women showed sass. They allowed their true selves to shine through. That's how I try to be with the people I work with. I call it wearing your heart on your sleeve. People always know I'm being real with them. They respect it.

As Roger says it, "Soul is . . . an unwillingness to bend in those directions which don't feel right because to do so is to deny the existence of a cultural style and integrity."

Do You with honesty. Be strong in your sense of who you are. Brand yourself and unleash your Soul Power.

Be True to Yourself

It can't be fake. You can't suddenly decide you're going to go from being a preppy white college kid to a homeboy with baggy jeans. Please don't go from a buttoned-down Oxford to an oversized Knicks jersey and chains just because you want to be cool and part of the hip-hop culture. Not being yourself is not hip hop. You won't gain any cool points. People will pierce right through your flimsy armor.

When you're trying to be somebody else, when you don't realize what you're good at, and you want to be everything to everybody, you'll be nothing to yourself.

But if you are the nerd who's great with numbers and has a degree in accounting who happens to love the music business, you could find your fit in hip hop without contriving some image for yourself that's not truly who you are.

Mignon Espy, formerly Def Jam's vice president of sales, couldn't be anyone but Mignon. She gets called "the chocolate-covered white girl." She doesn't care. She'll go on wearing her little Chanel suits while everyone around her lets it hang out, because that's her true style. Mignon is what she is—that fancy girl from a middle-class southern family who went to the best schools.

But Mignon loves this business. She was made for it. She keeps it real. She has the brassy attitude and mouth that allowed her to hold her own at any Def Jam meeting. She doesn't try to be what she's not. That authenticity makes her better at what she does, because she has a natural-born capacity to translate the hip-hop music world to those mainstream merchandisers at Wal-Mart and Target. Mignon speaks both languages. That's why I took her with me to Warner.

For years, Def Jam had Lyor, an Israeli CEO with a crew cut and his own distinct middle-aged hipster style! The label's new CEO, L.A. Reid, wears impeccably tailored Italian designer suits and has his staff call him Mr. Reid. He's not trying to conform. Why should he? L.A. has been doing L.A. successfully for decades. I respect him for that.

Authenticity translates into honesty. The people I respect the most in this business are the ones who can admit when there is a job that's not right for them. We can't all be Derek Jeter. Every team needs a good third baseman. Admitting that a particular task is not within your capabilities, or that somebody might be better for a job, is a sign of maturity and loyalty to the team.

In his book *From Good to Great*, Jim Collins likens a business to passengers on a bus. Not only do you need the right number of people riding that bus, you need the right people in the right seats if it's going to move forward. The good passengers willingly give up a seat if it's not for them. They know it's the only way to get to the next stop.

When Deidre Graham first started out at Def Jam's West Coast office in Los Angeles, she was just a green kid with next to no work experience. She didn't really know what her particular brand was, or what she was good at. She just had a general desire to be in the entertainment business.

We didn't give her any specific marching orders. I liked her spirit, but I had no idea what she could do. If you recall, I just told her to pick up the keys and show up the next day. She sat on the reception desk and started answering the phones, even though it was clear the others in the office resented her being there.

She was the voice on the other end of the phone, so she had the direct line of communication to the New York office. We liked her phone manner. Gradually, we started piling the work on. We gave her a party to organize for LL Cool J. We gave her a $5,000 budget and told her to go to it.

"I didn't know who to call or where to go, or what type of venue would be right, so I just started busting my ass, driving around L.A., checking out all the hot spots," she told me later.

She found a place and filled it with the who's who of Los Angeles. The TV show *In the House* was in its second season, and she got all the heads of NBC there. She did a "fly away with deejays" contest to hype LL's presence, and managed to get it all done under budget. From that point on I put her in charge of all the West Coast events.

Deidre juggled the responsibilities of receptionist, office manager and events coordinator. When something needed to get done, she didn't throw her hands up in the air and say she didn't know how. True to the spirit of hip hop, she used her imagination and figured out how to make it happen.

She became the go-to girl. Whenever I came to town, she

took care of everything. The artists loved her because she'd hook them up with whatever they wanted. She'd take them to swap meets and clubs, or just hang out with them in the studio.

But we wanted to see what else we could do. The local radio rep we had was getting kind of lazy, so we put her in charge of that too. She had to do promotions, visit with the program directors and go on interviews.

Deidre hated it. She didn't complain. She worked it as best she could, but schmoozing with radio executives just wasn't her thing. Deidre wasn't able to do Deidre in that position. After ten months of kissing ass the radio stations still weren't playing our records, and the music was good.

She finally let me know her frustration and I couldn't fault her for that because I knew she'd tried. We brought her up to work in New York and found her something better to do. Eventually, she worked up to senior vice president of marketing.

Find Your Fit

Appearance and manners, while important, are just the icing on the cake. Once you've made that first impression, there's a way to do you that goes much deeper.

You have to deliver the substance with the style. In business, staying power is earned. It's all about your performance and that special brand of service that you bring. Be an individual, but please don't be individualistic. Stand out for a purpose that's bigger than you. You have to find your fit within the organization as a whole.

Look at the people around you. Look at the landscape of the day. Now ask yourself, "What can I do better than them?" "What does the business need more of that I can offer?" "What separates me?"

When I first started out at Def Jam, I wondered how I was going to be a complement to the team. I wanted to be an asset. I wanted to be noticed for my work, and for how I picked up the slack of others.

Russell Simmons was the godfather of hip hop. He was the muse who inspired the artists. He was the man who created this company that develops and sells our culture to the world. That spot was taken! Lyor was architect and overseer. He had the vision and he drew up the master plans.

So what could I add to the mix?

I had two things going for me: a brain for business and the artistic credibility of a former rapper. I could talk to the rap artists because I was one of them and I understood their struggle. I live and breathe music. I can go into a studio and tell any artist how to make it better and they will listen to me because they know I've walked their walk. To them I'm not just some corporate asshole who only wants to sell records.

But I'm also a details guy. Mom was an accountant. I studied engineering. To execute the vision and sell the product you need marketing plans, demographic surveys, a budget. I understood how to motivate people and keep them in line. I knew about all of that from my days of overseeing hundreds of people at World Connections Travel.

I was that guy who knew how to dot the *i*'s and cross the *t*'s.

At that time, no one else at Def Jam had my kind of hands-on managerial experience. Few people at the company back then had the discipline of a formal education. Most of the guys in the office were homeboys from Hollis who were just along for the ride. Sure, they may have helped Russell back in the day, but I didn't see them getting any work done when I came on board.

Life at Def Jam was one big party. One guy used to get so stoned he'd stay slumped over his desk for hours. This was a

$30 million company that had the potential to be a $400 million company, but they needed a Kevin Liles to help blast it off and turn it into a professional organization. From this day forth I knew my mission: build a team that can fully serve the organization's day to day operations and fuel its growth initiatives.

That sounds pretty bold coming from a twenty-three-year-old kid from Baltimore. But by the time a paying gig as Def Jam's mid-Atlantic promotions manager came up in 1993, I'd already been interning for free for two years. From where I sat I had a pretty good idea of where the gaps were, and how to fill them. I knew the organization had to become more professional.

I'd already invested a lot of my own money showing them that I was their man. Whatever they needed to get done, I'd do it without asking for anything in return. One time, Russell came to town and needed several new pairs of Adidas. I couldn't really afford it, but I used money from my own pocket to buy them for him and personally delivered them to his hotel to demonstrate that I was the guy who could make it happen.

I made it my business to know all the answers about sales and distribution. I was plugged in to all the other regional offices, so I knew what went down in all the meetings and conference calls from Chicago to Miami. I would stay late in the office in case Russell or Lyor called, so I would be the one to answer the phone. If they needed information, I would be the one in the building with the answer.

I did the stuff that nobody else wanted to do. I used to spend thousands of dollars of my own money on mail-outs. I did whatever it took to make a Def Jam event in my region a success. I can't count how many times I drove all night to be somewhere and slept in the car.

I was all about getting it done and asking for nothing in return. I was grooming myself to run point for the team.

But I was still in Baltimore. Other than the guy who answers the phone, Russell didn't know who the hell I was. I could not assume that when a full-time, paying job came open that I would be the one to get it. I'd given them two free years of my time, but I knew there'd be a long line of people I'd have to compete with, so I had to figure out a way to cut that first impression when I finally had their face-to-face attention.

I figured everyone would show up for their interviews in jeans and sneakers. So I did what any engineering student fresh out of school would do when they interview for a job. I put on a suit and headed to New York.

I was prepared. I had a concertina file and briefcase crammed full of demographic charts. I had all the material I needed to show them how we were doing in the mid-Atlantic markets, and what we needed to do better. I could tell them what record stores we were in, which clubs paid us, which radio deejays loved us. I knew all the spin statistics of every artist, and exactly what we needed to do to get the play.

When I got to the Def Jam headquarters, which back then were downtown at 280 Elizabeth Street in the days when drug dealers, not French bistros, owned the corner, I was shocked. The elevator was decorated in graffiti and blood spatters. Cardboard boxes of vinyl were lined up along the hallways and piled on the only conference table in the office. I knew there was a window, but you couldn't see daylight behind the cartons of records that had to be shipped out to the stores.

The president's office was just a 100-square-foot hole. Desks were in the middle of the hallway. Maybe there was some method in the madness, but it sure was madness.

I thought, "This is the Almighty Def Jam?"

There were a bunch of guys I'd never seen before waiting to go into the office. I wondered, "Who are these people? I've never seen them in the street and I know everyone there is to know in

D.C. and Baltimore. How is it that they are interviewing for this job?"

They were no more impressed with me. Dave Harleston, who was the president in those days, peppered me with tough questions. Lyor Cohen, who was Run DMC's road manager at the time, gave me one of his cold hard stares. They were looking at me like, "Who is this clown in the suit?"

Lyor, a man of few words, asked me, "Are you sure you know what the f___ you are doing?"

But I showed them stuff they'd never seen before. I knew I'd killed them. They *had* to hire me because they had to elevate their game and become a more full-service organization. Compared to who was already working there, I was in a class of my own.

After I was hired, the promotions came fast. I leapfrogged over people directly above me because I'd carved out specialties for myself. I wasn't about duplicating the efforts of others and competing to get attention, I was out there on my own inventing better ways to do things for the evolution of the team.

I got us play on the radio stations by putting myself at the disposal of program directors. I schmoozed everyone, from the interns to the deejays, because I knew that people in the lower ranks were the ones who got things done and they'd remember me for the respect I showed them. Some of those same keepers run the radio industry today and they *still* remember. It's good karma that comes back again and again when I'm trying to get a few spins for an artist's new album or when, like the other day at Hot 97, the artists are more than an hour late and show up smelling like weed!

I built up street teams from scratch. I went out of pocket to blow up events at college campuses and clubs. No one was doing street teams like we were. I wasn't just hiring kids off the street to hand out flyers. We'd take over the place with poster boards in subways, phone booths, bus stops. I'd have them throw parties in the parking lot at a radio summer jam and take over the joint. We even had skywriters!

I found college kids and groomed them to be future Def Jam employees. Our street team was made up of the smart, ambitious students who wanted to make it in the music industry.

My love for the brand, Def Jam, became synonymous with how I branded myself. I ate, breathed and dreamed Def Jam. It was flowing in my veins. While I was still true to myself, Kevin Liles became the brand with the mouth. As Lyor would always say, "Base all your decisions on the logo. Ask yourself if it's good for the logo." Everyone in the company adopted the philosophy.

Big Pimpin'

Not literally, unless that's your particular hustle. By pimp I mean that, once you've found your groove and figured out how to Do You, you've got to go all out. Just like the hip-hop artist or athlete who soups up his new Escalade with the chrome rims, 400-amp stereo systems, suede seats or furry dice, you've also got to customize yourself—within reason!

Once you find your niche and a way to brand yourself, expand on it, full-blown. The most successful people know how to evolve in what they do. Even the specialists have to continually reinvent themselves and build new skills if they are going to stay hot and on top of their game.

The artists with staying power are the ones who have expanded their brand. LL Cool J is in his thirties. Some may feel that's old in the world of rap, but he's done television shows, he's made movie appearances and his latest album, *Definition*, is solid platinum. Jay-Z retired from rap to become a business entrepreneur. He already owns a club, 40/40, in Manhattan and has his fingers in many other lucrative sidelines. P. Diddy's doing his Sean Jean clothing line and who knows what next.

Def Jam the brand would not be what it is today if we didn't push the envelope and try new things. Def Jam represents newness. We are a culture of explorers. We can and should push the boat. These days, gaming sales are outpacing CD sales in the hip-hop market, so we started a gaming division with Electronic Arts.

Universal Music Group owns the brand for music publishing and recording music, but Russell, Lyor and I own the rights to the brand for anything else we choose to diversify into. Today we're involved in television shows. We do live poetry performances on Broadway. We have a clothing line, Def Jam University. We've launched two video games. We grossed $100 million in less than a year just with one game, Def Jam Vendetta. Our latest venture is Def Jam Mobile. Cell phones are perfect products for the Def Jam brand as they become a portable means of self-expression.

Expanding our brand shows the kids in our culture, the consumer, that "Wow, anything is possible."

Kids want to fight the power. Instead of just being a corporate establishment, we want to give them that power by seeing our example and knowing that they have the tools to go out and do the things they want to do.

Of course, we have to stick with what works for our core brand. In entertainment and for many consumer goods, there are plenty of directions we could go. It might be hard for Colgate to get into records, or for Pepsi to sell motorcycles. I don't necessarily see us selling ink-jet printers. Much depends on how strong your identity is to start with.

Frank Ski, Atlanta's "King of Morning Show Radio" and my homeboy from Baltimore, is a hot personality in his region right now. He's signed on with an advertising agency and now his face is all over the billboards of Atlanta selling Big Macs. He's doing cameos in movies. He's planning on opening a club.

Frank admits he is getting a little old for a deejay whose major market is women in their late teens and early twenties. But he's building the skills he needs to be current with the tastes of a much younger audience by hiring young interns. He's learning all about digital music so that he can explore what's out there and be more efficient.

To get the radio ratings he needs, he has to market himself in a way that makes listeners not only recognize who he is, but go to the trouble of filling out the ratings form and saying exactly why they like the *Frank Ski Show*. Splashing his image all over town can't hurt.

Frank's been at the radio game for more than twenty years, but he doesn't just sit back and let his reputation carry him. I tease him for being the poster boy for McDonald's. But Frank's response is, "Kevin, there's a season for everyone. When you're hot you're hot and you have to make the most of it."

Be like Frank. Don't miss your season and spend the rest of your career chasing what should have been yours.

 RULE 2

What: Do You

Why: Once you've found your will you have to package it and present it to the world.

How: Pick a flava. Find a style that expresses your personality, from the way you tie your shoelaces to the way you handle your business. Do it with polish. Rich or poor, there's no excuse for being grimy and bad-mannered.

But: Don't be fake. Make sure what you put out there is real and not just some cheap counterfeit of someone else's brand.

Walk This Way

We are born weak, we need strength; helpless we need

aid; foolish we need reason. All that we lack at birth, all

that we need when we come to man's estate, is the gift of

education.

—Jean-Jacques Rousseau

You've found your will, now you have to find a way. Make sure it's the right way. Find the knowledge, hone the skills and learn the lessons you need to execute the plan.

There are many ways to learn. One of them is college. Formal education can teach you the basics and open up your mind. It lays a foundation so you *can* think about the possibilities beyond flipping burgers at Burger King or hanging out on the corner. It gives you the discipline to meet deadlines. It provides you with a safe environment to take risks.

Potential employers like to see that you have a degree just to see that you can finish what you started. Sometimes it's hard to get any employer to look at you without that piece of paper, whether it's from the lowliest community college or Harvard.

If you choose to be a lawyer or a doctor or some other type of professional looking to work at a top firm or practice, for sure the right school helps. For that tiny minority of the privileged or the gifted, the letters next to the name are often a prerequisite for making your way and competing in the marketplace.

Joe Haskins, the CEO of Harbor Bank in Baltimore, loaded up on degrees. As a black man coming up in the civil rights era, he decided he had to be better and more qualified than his white counterparts. He graduated from Morgan State University in Baltimore in 1971, moved on to New York University Business School, attended graduate school at Johns Hopkins to study political science and economics, then got himself an advanced business degree from Wharton.

Joe admits that all those degrees might not have been necessary for his ultimate success. But "I didn't want to give anyone the excuse that I am not qualified because I lack the education," he says.

Lacking the advantage of a formal education is no excuse for not succeeding either. It's on you to be better informed and more accomplished than the rich kid who went to Yale. You can still read, watch the news and pick up a newspaper and be ready with something intelligent to say to a prospective employer.

You have the power to bust it wide open, degree or no degree. Once you're inside the building, it's more street smarts than a college degree that determines whether you make it in the business world. Education is no substitute for life experience. You don't learn how to go on a date with someone by reading a book on a theory of dating.

It wouldn't hurt, and may even help, to follow Joe's lead. Don't give them an excuse not to hire you if you can help it. But if you haven't had the opportunity to go to college, or financial circumstances prevented you from completing the courses, take heart. Some of the biggest leaders in business were dropouts. In fifteen years, I don't recall being asked where I went to school. I left Morgan State seventeen credits shy of my engineering degree. It hasn't held me back.

No one cares that Bill Gates dropped out in his junior year at Harvard in 1975. In between classes, he'd started his own business, Microsoft, with a childhood friend. He created a version of the programming language BASIC for the first microcomputer.

Even at that age, Gates had a vision that the computer would be a valuable tool on every office desktop and in every home. At the time, everyone thought it was a wack move. But it was the smartest decision he could have made. He started developing software for personal computers and now he's one of the richest men in the world. He changed the course of history. How could college have taught him to do that?

I first met Bill Gates when we were doing a press conference together in Los Angeles. I was there with LL Cool J to demonstrate the new MSN program. By using LL, the very opposite of a computer nerd, we were making the point that the program was user-friendly and cool.

I decided to corner the man for ten minutes before the event. I wanted to meet him in person to feel his spirit and learn something. We spoke a little about the troubles of the music industry and digital downloading. He told me how he'd predicted the slump in music sales and piracy problems five years before it happened.

I was blown away. It was like he was physically here today, but his mind was already in 2010. He had his own special genius that can't be shaped by a classroom inside some leafy East Coast ivory tower. Back in the '70s, he was already operating in the next century. He had the kind of vision that comes from thinking outside the box of a formal education.

Not everyone can be a Bill Gates, but his example shows us that going to a good college and getting a degree doesn't guarantee that you will get paid. If Bill had stayed in school, he'd have wasted two more years that he could have devoted to his entrepreneurial journey. Somebody else might have gotten a jump on the technology.

As a matter of fact, Steve Ballmer, Microsoft's CEO, lived down the hall from Bill in his college dorm. What if he'd started a rival company that left Microsoft in the dust? When it's your season, it's your season. You have to act.

So now I'm going to say something to you that's going to make every parent hate me. If an opportunity comes along before you get that piece of paper, take it! Just make sure it's a great opportunity you can build on for the long term if you're going to take the step of quitting college.

It's better to graduate if you are able to, no question. But if the school of life has an opening, jump right in. What counts is not so much where you learn, but what you learn. Just make sure you finish what you started, even if it's later on in life.

E Squared

Life is full of opportunities to learn if you're open to them. Education and experience can be one and the same. I call it E squared.

J.-J. Rousseau, the dead French guy I quoted at the top of this chapter, revolutionized the concept of education back in the 18th century, when even the most elementary kind of formal schooling was only available to the elite ruling classes.

Rousseau had no formal education. He was a terrible teacher. He was so broke he couldn't bring up his own children. But he understood that education comes from the environment we live in, the example of other people and our own discovery of the way of the world.

The key is to create opportunities for new experiences, then to stop and reflect on what those experiences teach us. You learn by doing. My life is my classroom. When I was at Morgan State University, my greatest learning experiences came when I was on tour with my rap group.

I'll never forget the day I went up to New York to get on the radio with Red Alert, a deejay who helped make hip hop popular. We drove all night and slept outside the studio so that we could be on his show the next morning. Being there, watching him do his thing, seeing what records he chose to spin and how he could vibe with the artists and translate that for the listener was a huge revelation to me at the time. Uncle Red showed me how it's done and gave me hope.

My experience at World Connections Travel from the ages of seventeen to twenty-two taught me how to lead, organize and manage more than four hundred individuals from very different backgrounds. Their job was to sell travel deals and luxury vacations over the phone. To do that you need a force of highly motivated people hungry to make a sale.

Jim Buckingham, my boss at the time, showed me how you can fire people up by posting inspirational slogans like "Make It Happen" all over the office cubicles and walls. He'd remind the telemarketers of the importance of a pleasant phone manner by sticking Post-it notes on their headsets. He showed me how the offer of a reward, like a free trip or cash bonus to employees who hit a certain volume of calls, could inspire them. At the beginning of each shift, we would give a twenty-minute pep talk to our staff. We had to get their mind in the right state for the job. We had to pump them up.

There are certain things about the corporate world that are best learned by the trial and error of experience. When Jay-Z first started out in the business, he didn't know a whole lot about how things worked. Jay's one of the sharpest entrepreneurs I know, but back in the day he was raw from the street. The music business was just another hustle for him.

In 1996, when he put out the song "Ain't No N____s" featuring Foxy Brown on his label, Roc-A-Fella, he was desperate to get some spins on national radio. Back then I was vice president of promotions. People knew me as the king of radio. I had the connections that could get any song played. Wise guy Irv "Gotti" Lorenzo advised Jay to come to my office and bribe me! Irv knew perfectly well that I had too much integrity to play it that way; he was just messing with Jay.

I was in the middle of a conference call when Jay and his partners, Damon Dash and Biggs Burke, walked in with a huge paper bag full of cash. They placed the bag of bills on top of my desk and asked me to help them get their record played. Jay said, "Kevin, just do what you do." I said, "Jay, I like your song, but that's not how we do things around here!"

I decided to help him not because of the money, but because there was something special about Jay and his crew. I handed him back the bag, and the rest is music-making history.

Today, Jay's got the right corporate moves down. Not too long ago, this same guy was rubbing shoulders with the Prince of Wales in England. He looked every inch the English gentleman in a perfectly tailored suit and not a word or gesture out of place. Jay-Z learned how to up his game by watching other people and interacting with executives in the mainstream business world. Not only was he a product of his environment, he was becoming a product of experience. Jay was, and still is, a quick study of life.

Get Educated

Even though I didn't graduate, I'm still in school. My education never stopped. I've been studying at Def Jam University and the Kevin Liles Continuing Education College of Life. Every time I learn something new, I get a rush. Why would I ever want to put a stop to that?

If I don't know something, I'm not afraid to admit it and ask. I keep a big-ass dictionary on my desk, so when I stumble on a word I've never heard before, I look it up, type it in my Blackberry and make sure I use it correctly in a sentence a few times. This way I expand my vocabulary daily.

Whatever I need to know, I do the research to find out. Whether that means book learning, asking someone with the expertise or searching the Internet, I make sure I find out everything I can about a subject before I jump in.

I'm not saying don't go to college. If you can, if you have the access and it's your best opportunity to learn, do it. If you haven't had the advantage growing up, promise yourself and a prospective employer that you'll take a few courses at a community college, through a correspondence school or online to build the skills. Depending on the industry you choose to go into, you may have to. Either way, it shows you've got the will and you'll need the extra hustle to outshine the college grads.

There's a reason why hip-hop entrepreneurs give back to the community by funding scholarships. Me, Ludacris, Russell, Snoop, etc., we all want to give kids the access and opportunity so many of us never had when we were growing up. We recognize it's important. But don't chase a degree just because you think it's part of a formula for success. Do it with purpose. Be guided by your own will for success, not your parents' expectations or desires.

I'm definitely not saying don't finish high school. Please, *please* get your GED, no matter what. At least learn the basics. You don't have to stay ignorant, no matter how poor or unstable your come-up was. Anyone can study up on the fundamentals.

The importance of getting educated was drummed into me from the time I could walk and talk. My mother sacrificed everything so that she could go to college and get her accounting degree.

My birth father left us when me and my younger brother were just babies. With no one to provide for us, we all moved into my grandmother's house. In those early years, we were raised by our grandparents. We survived on welfare, while my mother went to night school and worked a day job to support us.

She was determined to graduate at the top of her class. Her first-year finals were a week before she was about to give birth to my baby brother. Mom scored in the 90th percentile in advanced accounting. Because she had to work so hard for it, she was determined that she was going to give us a chance at going to college without having to go through the same hell and sacrifice to get there.

So I mean it when I say GET EDUCATED. To suggest anything less would disrespect my mother and all that she worked for. Find some way, any way, even if you can't afford college and you don't have your mom to kick your ass!

Information Is Power

I didn't always appreciate my opportunities to acquire knowledge. I coasted in school. I had no worries or distractions at home. I was lucky. My parents stood over me until I got my homework done. In elementary school I was the quiet kid who knew how to please the teachers.

I liked learning. I was good at math and I had a natural talent for writing that made me good at English. But I put forth just enough effort to glide through with B's and the occasional A. By high school, I started discovering more things outside the classroom I liked to do. I was intrigued by life on the streets, so hanging out, playing football on the field next to my house and roaming the neighborhood became distractions from homework.

I still pulled off the grades, but now I was scraping by on B's and C's. I didn't really care. I was having too much fun with my homeboys. But then my high school social studies teacher, Joe Woodfolk, took an interest. He saw me as somebody who wasn't living up to his potential. In my junior and senior years, Mr. Woodfolk, an old-school, civil rights–era man of intellect who believes in the power of education for African-American kids, got me hooked on books.

He made me read up on history and ideas. In his classroom I learned about Rousseau's *Social Contract*. Rousseau's ideas about the rights of the people and empowerment through education gave me the motivation to do something with my life.

Mr. Woodfolk introduced me to the autobiography of Malcolm X. He made me read the speeches of Martin Luther King Jr. He got me to read *Native Son* by Richard Wright and *Beloved* by Toni Morrison.

Later in life, out of habit, I introduced myself to self-help books like Robert Kiyosaki's *Rich Dad, Poor Dad*, which made me understand that acquiring wealth and building success is possible for anyone no matter where they are from. He opened me to the world and the ideas that have shaped who I am today through book reading.

I already had the gift of the gab, but something happens to you when you discover the power of words. Reading isn't just for acquiring the basic knowledge and skills for success. It's how you learn about yourself and the life beyond your corner.

When you read Nelson Mandela's *Long Walk to Freedom*, you feel his struggle with apartheid and you can relate it to your own burdens, whatever they may be. When you read the wisdom and courage of Martin Luther King Jr.'s words, you discover the power of your own voice.

In business, we rely heavily on the power of the word. We use our powers of self-expression to sell, persuade, make a case and negotiate a deal. We gain our edge and build up our arsenal of words through the language of books.

This is especially true in the hip-hop industry. We're selling the rhymes that can inspire and stir up emotions. Our best rap artists are our most literate poets. Language is our raw material. When we say "Word," we mean "Truth."

Whether we operate quietly behind the scenes to get things done, or we're out there in front pushing a product or performing a few rhymes, we have the confidence to make it happen because we have the vocabulary we need to express who we are. It's up to you to find the power between the pages.

Choose a Course

Besides getting me into the reading habit, Mr. Woodfolk steered me onto a path he believed would guarantee my future.

I was good in math. I was great at problem solving. He figured I ought to take advantage of these talents by choosing a secure profession. By my senior year in high school he convinced me to work toward becoming an engineer. He got me enrolled in a summer course right after my high school graduation that would earn me a scholarship and a spot in the engineering program at Morgan State University founded by NASA.

It seemed like a logical move at the time. Back then my idea of success was a steady job and a big enough paycheck to support my family. You can't get more nine-to-five than an electrical engineering job in the government. I even apprenticed that summer at the Maryland State Highway Administration.

But by the time I started my freshman year at Morgan, my band Numarx was on a roll. We'd already put out a couple of singles and we were touring all over the East Coast. Studying at the university was interesting to me for a while, but it became just one of several activities I was pursuing.

I had so many things going on in my junior year. I had the supervisor's job at World Connections Travel, where I'd started out as a telemarketer. I was more excited showing up for work and learning about management and marketing from my boss Jim Buckingham than showing up for physics class.

I had my various hustles going on with friends. I was running a local street team, selling and getting vinyl played for various record labels, including our own, Marx Bros., and Def Jam. When I wasn't on tour I was partying and staying in local hotels where me and my crew could have the kind of fun you can't have when you're still living at your parents' house.

For a while I got away with it. Because I was in one of the hottest local bands, kids on campus wanted to be in with the cool crowd. I got people to do my homework for me and tape the lectures that I missed. But by the beginning of my senior year at college it was clear that something had to give. I was so stretched that I wasn't getting much of an education out of any of the activities I was pursuing.

I started to do fewer things. No matter how many willing classmates I had to write my papers for me, they couldn't sit in on my exams. The more advanced the courses got, the worse my grades got. I lost my scholarship with just a few months to go before graduation.

I was at a crossroads. I could give up all the extracurricular activities that truly excited and challenged me and knuckle down on the course work. I could get myself thousands of dollars into debt to pay the rest of my tuition so that I could graduate to become an engineer who earns a steady paycheck. But did I really care?

Nope.

I probably would have made a good engineer if I'd applied myself, but it didn't excite me enough to learn more about it. I was already making $50,000 a year at my marketing job, plus extra from performing with my rap group. My mother was working her whole life to make $50,000. I decided I didn't need a piece of paper to exceed my salary expectations.

Of all the tough decisions I'd had to make in my young life, this was a killer. As I sat up in my room in my parents' house, trying to concentrate on writing a term paper on the computer my mother paid for, I knew how much my leaving school would disappoint her and my father, not to mention Mr. Woodfolk! I was the first of my family to ever go to university, and here I was, close to the finish line, walking away.

But my mind was on the music. I was beginning to feel like every minute spent in class was time wasted. I was in a hurry to pursue my true passion. I couldn't finish just to finish and do whatever my parents thought was best for me. Their priorities weren't wrong, but they weren't right for me.

My mother put the pressure on. She was still sore from the time I decided to drop out of Boy Scouts when I was fifteen. (She had me in lockdown for a month after that. She still keeps the part of my uniform covered in merit badges somewhere in the house.) If she was mad that I never finished Eagle Scouts, not finishing college nearly put her over the edge.

But I had to do what I knew was best for me. I said "Okay, I've got enough education, now I'm ready to go out and make mistakes in the real world."

She still loved me, but the purse strings were cut from the moment I told her I was quitting. My parents were deeply disappointed. They were trying to mold me by putting certain constraints on me, but they didn't have to live my life. I had to ask myself, whether it was a degree or another Scouts badge, what difference would either make in my life? I already understood the principles of accountability, teamwork and collaboration. I had the basics down cold. What else was there to learn? It was time to walk it and talk it.

Degrees Are for Doing

Even though I didn't finish college, I respect the highly educated among us. People who've taken the time to learn everything there is to know about a subject and get all of those degrees demonstrate that they have the discipline to focus and dive deep into something. Knowledge is great, but it's what you do with that knowledge that makes the difference and makes things happen.

This subject heats me up. My baby sister Tiffany, for example, came to me the other day to ask for my financial help so that she can do her master's in computer science.

But when I asked her what she planned to do when she got her MA, Tiffany, who's twenty-four, just shrugged and said, "I don't know, I might start up a car wash with some friends."

I'm proud of her. There aren't many young black women who can say they have advanced degrees in this field. But I responded by saying, "What the hell! My homeboys can do that and they don't need no master's degrees!"

I was trying to make her understand that if she's going to spend that much time in school, she'd better justify it to me with how she lives her life. She'd better mentor other young women who may not have the same opportunity, and help open the door to a profession that advances their economic status.

You don't spend thousands of dollars and years of your life to study for studying's sake. People who make a career out of school aren't well rounded and often don't want to face the world outside of academia. If you were blessed enough to have the opportunity to learn that much, you've got to take that invaluable knowledge and use it in real life for the betterment of mankind. You've got to pay it forward.

It Ain't for Everyone

I can name dozens of people inside and outside of Def Jam who made it in the business without getting that piece of paper from a university. But to ensure their success they made certain they had the skills to offer and the ability and desire to constantly learn, degree or no degree.

Consider the early career path of Tishawn Gayle, product manager at Def Jam.

It was the winter of 1996 when Tishawn started at the label. He was studying computer science at Northeastern University in Boston, then switched to business school to do a double major in management information systems and marketing. Somehow Tishawn made his grades in class, but in our college rep program he found the major he loved.

It was Tishawn's job to advance awareness of the brand at the college and street level on campuses from Massachusetts up into Vermont. As an unpaid intern on our street team, he had to push all of our new and current releases in school newspapers and on campus radio stations, through parties and campus promotions.

He organized other kids to pass out flyers at the student center. He designed his own marketing campaign to let everybody know when a new album was coming out. He helped us blow up the exposure of a new Foxy Brown album and got us plenty of play on college radio stations from Buffalo to Boston.

The job was all-consuming and not exactly lucrative for a guy with school fees and rent to pay, but Tishawn was the cool guy on campus. He had a little of the computer nerd thing going on, but he could meet girls because, he says, "I was with Def Jam. I was at all the happening places letting everybody know what was going on. I was the man!"

Tishawn was good at it. The skills he was getting at Northeastern were giving him the edge over all the other regional college reps. He could design graphics and organize his game plan on the computer. He knew the basics of marketing, and how to maximize his impact on campus. His education helped.

But what was just a way to party and indulge his love of music eventually became his mission. He saw me speak at one of my road shows, dressed like the college kids and knowing the lingo but still being corporate. Tishawn was a hip-hop kid, and I was too.

Later on, Tishawn told me that was a turning point for him.

"Kevin, you were that guy. You let us know that at Def Jam it's okay to be ourselves. This is how we get down. We can dress in street clothes. We can curse. This is what our artists are, this is what I am, this is how we are able to sell these records. Because there is a direct link between us, our artists and our fans. When I saw you on that podium I thought, 'Goddamn! This is it!' "

Tishawn could see himself standing where I was standing. He turned down paying internships managing information systems so he could stay in the music industry. He knew how rare a thing it was to get a foot in the door at a leading record label, doing something he loved.

Knowing he had to be in the mix in the daytime, he hustled for us while he scraped by in school. After grinding for two years and networking like crazy to build relationships with our executives, Tishawn joined our sales and distribution team.

He enrolled at Northeastern because it offered a co-op program, alternating six months of work experience with six months of course work. It just so happened that his work experience started breaking away from what was in his course work. But he got his money's worth out of the program. It taught him the most valuable lesson of all.

"You've got to be about the business in life, even when you're in school," he says.

Like Tishawn, Tina Davis, who was Def Jam's head of A&R, started at college with a different career path in mind. She'd always had an ear for music. When Tina got good grades in school, her daddy would reward her with something. First she asked for piano lessons, then she asked for guitar lessons, violin lessons, drums and a piano. But to her, music was still just a hobby.

By the time she turned twenty-seven, Tina was lost. Growing up in L.A., she tried all kinds of odd jobs on the fringes of the entertainment industry, but she wasn't going anywhere. Indulgent parents made it easy for her to coast and she lacked the focus. So Tina decided to enroll at Grambling State University in Louisiana.

Tina majored in broadcast journalism. She was good in English and she was cute. She figured she had the right look and the necessary outgoing personality to be an anchor and a reporter. But it wasn't her passion. Soon she was spending most of her spare time deejaying on college radio and putting together college concerts and talent shows.

Erykah Badu was a classmate of Tina's. Since a good friend of Tina's was married to the senior vice president of A&R for Virgin Records, Tina made the introduction that helped Erykah get her first record deal.

"It felt good," Tina recalled. "I was like a little A&R person running around saying, 'I can get you signed,' not even realizing that what I was doing was A&R. It was at that point I realized I wanted to get into music."

Meanwhile, she'd hit a wall as far as school was concerned. Her grades were fine, but every time she signed her name on that student loan form, she'd think to herself, "Damn, here's another $3,000 I have to pay back."

By her senior year, the school administration discovered that Tina had a dad with the financial wherewithal to pay for her tuition. She was disqualified for a student loan. Broke and $50,000 in debt, she had to find some way to pay back what she owed and finance her last year in college. But Daddy pulled the plug. He figured it was time for Tina to learn to stand on her own two feet.

That crisis got Tina thinking about her life, what it all meant, and why in the hell she was putting herself in the debt hole for something she didn't feel much passion for. She started soul-searching to see what had led to this point.

She began to realize the one consistent thread running through it was music. She remembered back to the time she was in fourth grade and she'd charge the other kids five cents each to see her perform concerts at recess, singing Natalie Cole songs. Tina is the first to admit she can't sing that well, but she'd always been creative and knew a good sound when she heard it.

So she dropped out of college and got herself a job as an A&R assistant at Def Jam's West Coast office. "It's what God had planned for me all along," she said.

Tina and Tishawn both got something out of school, but it wasn't what they expected, and it wasn't related to what was in the academic program. They both learned something about themselves and what they wanted to do. School gave them the environment and an opportunity to take risks and make it happen. Tina and Tishawn supplied the courage.

Neither of them regrets going to college, and neither of them regrets dropping out. They got educated because they were open to the lessons and had the imagination to realize that the value wasn't always inside a textbook and the payoff wasn't necessarily a college credit.

"Formal education gave me choices and made me look into myself," Tina said. "It was one last hurrah before I became an adult, but it was also an education about how to be independent financially and in life."

Tina and Tishawn might not be where they are today if they hadn't gone to college. In fact, last summer Tishawn took night classes at Baruch College in New York City so that he could finally get his degree. But he says he's only doing it for his own personal satisfaction. Who knows, I might do the same one day, just to please my mom.

Even top executives who did get degrees got less education from the classroom than they did from campus life. I recently asked Doug Morris, the CEO of Universal Music Group, who did complete his bachelor of arts degree, whether he values his formal education. His answer: not so much.

"I faked my way through college," he said. " I was lucky I graduated. I did it because education was important to my parents and it was expected of all the kids in our family. But it never meant much to me. I don't remember a thing about the classes, trigonometry, geology or geometry."

The only thing Doug can recall from those days was the fun he had partying. It wasn't a waste of time, because he built the social connections he'd need later in life as he built his career in music. Lyor Cohen plugged into a similar network of people as head of his college concert committee, experience that would serve him well when he became road manager for Run DMC.

The takeaway from their experiences wasn't the academics. It was the training they got for life.

Listen to Learn

Everyone you meet along the way is going to have at least one important thing to teach you, if you're ready to hear it. Your mentors are going to be some of the most important people you'll ever know, so look out for them. Open up your ears, your mind and your heart.

You can have more than one mentor. In fact, you can have

dozens. Lyor Cohen and Russell Simmons are two of my great-est teachers, but they are just two on a long and growing list of people.

Your mentors won't all be equal. There are the friends and family you hold close who you can always turn to for a straight answer. Some show what they know by setting a great example. A rare few in life can be trusted implicitly. Others can teach you what not to do through their own bad example. Either way, they offer you the chance to study human nature and learn from life's experiences.

I've had some bad advice from people who pretended to have my best interests at heart. It's not always easy to tell at the time.

It happened when I was with Numarx. A guy in the music industry approached us claiming he could hook us up with the right people and help us take it to the next level. He called him-self an "advisor to the stars." We paid this asshole $10,000 for his services, but we ended up touring all over the East Coast and playing unpaid gigs in half-empty clubs.

My parents pleaded with me not to pay this guy. They didn't believe in handing over so much cash to someone who was basi-cally a stranger to us. But I sure as hell learned from him. By cheating me he taught me never to trust someone in business without at least doing a background check first.

Rod Halloman, one of my best friends back in Baltimore, taught me a lesson so important it helped define me as a person.

I couldn't have been more than twelve at the time. I was playing baseball on the blacktop lot near my house in Liberty Heights. I was pitching and Rod was hugging the plate, so I pitched like I had seen the professional players do on tele-vision. I threw the ball close to Rod so that he'd back up off the plate.

But Rod moved closer to the plate, daring me to try that

again. I did, and I hit him with the ball. It was a game, but he took it seriously. He walked up to the pitchers' mound and punched me in the face. I hardly knew him at the time. To me he was just some loudmouth kid. But when he decked me like that it taught me never to underestimate what anyone will do.

Some of the most powerful things I've learned in my career have come from the most unlikely of sources. I never thought a couple of crazy weedheads like rap artists Redman and Method Man would have something to teach me.

These are the same guys who refused to come out of the van when we had a radio show to do at one of the most important hip-hop stations because they were too busy smoking up. One time Red got so high on something that nobody could stop him from walking down the streets of our nation's capital in nothing but his briefs!

I was always the one trying to teach them and keep them in line. At times I resented all the craziness of artists. Their ass-hole stunts were wearing me out. Then in 1995, in the middle of my grind years at Def Jam, we were at the start of a concert tour in Pennsylvania when Red decided in the middle of his perfor-mance that he was going to jump up from a loudspeaker to a row of stage lights.

What he didn't know was that those lights were searing hot! I don't know what was going through his head to make him pull such a dumbass stunt, but he screamed and let go, falling at least twenty feet onto the stage, flat on his back. As he was lying there I thought to myself, "Oh no, oh crap, not on the first m____f___ing night!"

Red was passed out for a few seconds, and everything got all quiet. Then Meth rushed over to him and said over and over again, "Real n____s don't die, real n____s don't die! Get up Red! Come on, get up!"

Red got up and finished the performance, with a back full of bruises and third-degree burns on his hands. We had to take him to the hospital. After the show, he told me, "It took everything in my life to get up."

It was a stupid accident, but it showed me how much these artists give to their audiences. It didn't even occur to Redman not to get up off that stage floor. It made me realize that their dedication to their fans meant that I had to be equally dedicated to their well-being. It taught me how to take my role as caretaker and concierge to a whole new level. My motto became, "I am here to serve."

The "Isms"

I keep track of the wisdom I've learned from others in a file I call "The Isms." If you are planning to be part of an organization, listen out for them and write them down. Study the company's past and figure out how to use its philosophy to create your own isms.

"Anything is possible" is a Russell-ism. "Let your work speak for you" is a Lyor-ism. "Live and learn" is a Kevin-ism.

 **RULE 3**

What: Walk This Way

Why: Getting educated is *the* way to make it happen. Whether you study in college or the school of life, knowledge and experience will give you the tools you need for success.

How: Find a mentor, go to school, do the research, take notes, read. Open your mind.

But: Don't just follow the example of one teacher, one course or one book. Look for the lessons in everything, good or bad. Even a lousy example can teach you what not to do, or how to do it better.

Create a Blueprint

I'll tell you the difference between me and them

They trying to get they ones, I'm trying to get those Ms

One million, two million, three million . . .

—Jay-Z, "U Don't Know"

Wherever you've decided to go on your career path, you have to map out the best route to get there. Make a plan. Keep a blueprint for success in your head and on your hard drive. You may not always stick to it exactly, but it will serve to remind you why you've got your grind on and help you set your goals.

Some people like to make five-year plans. They say to themselves, "In 2010, I'm going to be vice president of marketing, and I'm going to have a three-bedroom house and two cars." That's crazy to me. Why limit yourself?

As much as I believe in planning for your future, I equally believe in living your best life now. As said best by Joel Olsteen, author of *Your Best Life Now*, "Happy, successful, fulfilled individuals have learned how to live their best lives now. They make the most of the present moment and thereby enhance their future."

There's a big difference between building an overall vision of what you want to achieve in a lifetime, and tying yourself down to one path. Your never know: the surprises along the way might turn out to be better than what you've drawn up for yourself.

Either way, you can't schedule your life's mission. Anything worth hustling for tends to take longer than the deadline you set for yourself. You can't know if the industry you chose to go into is going to go through a recession and leave hundreds of people jobless. You can't predict how new technology might completely change the future direction of a company. You can't control the future.

Instead, let planning become part of the way you go about your daily business. Dwight D. Eisenhower said, "In preparing for battle I have always found that plans are useless, but planning is indispensable." That means live for today and plan for tomorrow.

I'm always focused 100 percent on whatever task I have in front of me. But at the same time there's a little voice in the back of my head that's constantly trying to figure out where this moment fits into the overall vision. Like the dead president says, operate in the trenches, but always think about what's going to help you in the battle ahead.

That's what I call good planning. It's the true spirit of entrepreneurialism. The best entrepreneurs—whether they are running a business on their own or operating within a company—are constantly churning it over to see how ideas can be an opportunity.

If someone says to me, "Hey Kev, I see people are downloading their favorite tunes on their cell phones," my mind immediately starts to thinking, "How can I bring this to market? How can this enhance the brand? Who's going to benefit? Who will be the best partner in this?"

In fact, that's how a deal with American Greetings to create Def Jam Mobile came to fruition. We put our branding and wireless content onto cell phones. Today, Def Jam Mobile applications are displayed on thousands of square feet of retail space around the world. That same mind-set of thinking ahead and anticipating the opportunities made Def Jam's platinum-selling video game a reality.

Sure, the best entrepreneurs go by gut and instinct. But you don't get bigger and better by the seat of your pants alone. As Def Jam grew into the biggest hip-hop label in the world, it had to bring planning and forward thinking into its culture.

When I first joined the label, Def Jam didn't have some grand plan to grow into a large corporation, merge with some multinational media company, and move into the twenty-eighth floor of some glass and steel office tower in midtown Manhattan. We just wanted to get through the day and throw a hot party.

I think that's partly why Russell decided to make Lyor and me part of his team. He knew from the time I first started interning in Baltimore that I was always in the office, putting together weekly reports about which artists went to what venues and documenting how many times the local radio stations played our singles. No one else showed up for interviews at Def Jam's headquarters with color-coded pie charts breaking it down and showing which record stores were selling the most vinyl.

I had a concertina file full of Broadcast Data System, or BDS, reports. People may have laughed at me when I walked in with all that paperwork, but based on the information in those BDS printouts I could tell Russell which artists were getting the spins in our region, and where. I could tell him which radio program directors loved us, and who we needed to work on, and I had the numbers at my fingertips to back it up. Russell knew I had the vision and the blueprints that were necessary to turn Def Jam into a professional organization. He knew I was anal like that.

Keep One Eye Open

I don't claim to be smarter than anyone else. But when *you're* sleeping, *I've* got one eye open. By the time you wake up, I'm already ten steps ahead of you because with that one eye I've already decided what I want to do that day.

Everything has a purpose, from the way I lace my shoelaces to the tactics I choose when I'm putting together a record deal. Planning gives you the edge over the other guy, because you're always several moves ahead. You can anticipate what will go wrong, and how to fix it, or even switch to a Plan B, C or D if you have to. Like Warren Buffett said, "Noah didn't start building the ark when it was raining."

I expect the same forward thinking from the people I work with. If I give someone a budget of $300,000 for a project like a music video and they want another $200,000, they'd better have all the answers ready for me when I ask them exactly how that extra money is going to be spent. By the time they step into my office, they better know the return on investment and the risk to our profits without the additional investment.

The people who work under me have to justify and quantify their actions. They have to give me at least ten good ideas in case I don't like the first one. They have to come up with the list of what they're going to do and how they plan to execute it, and they have to have a backup plan in case, as almost always happens, the video shoot goes over budget.

It's crazy to me how many people don't think ahead. I'm the worst backseat driver because I'm always anticipating problems up the road. My old driver said I gave him a headache because I was always in his ear from behind, telling him to make lane changes to avoid accidents or traffic congestion.

I can't help myself. He had a lot to put up with, I'll give him that. But I've lost count of the number of times I was late for a meeting because he hadn't looked at a map and planned the route beforehand, or plugged the destination into the navigation system.

You just don't survive in the business world when you leave room for things to screw up. I demand that everyone who works for me be two weeks ahead of me. It may not always be possible, but the fact that they are even trying is going to be reflected in their performance.

Like it says in that book by Robin Sieger, *Natural Born Winners*, "Planning is as natural to the process of success as its absence is to the process of failure."

Always Be Prepared

You probably never would have guessed that a hip-hop executive could have been in the Boy Scouts. Well I was, for ten years. My mom was even a den mother. I was into it full-blown until I hit my teen years. By that time the uniforms started to feel kind of corny. But not before I'd taken the Scouts' science of planning to a whole new level.

Planning came into play when I was twelve and I had to earn my merit badge for surviving in the wilderness. They sent a team of us out to the Broad Creek Memorial Scout Reservation in Maryland and left us there to fend for ourselves over the weekend with nothing but a compass, a Swiss Army knife, some matches and the clothes on our backs. We had to find a safe, dry place to camp somewhere inside of two thousand acres of land.

I did what very few other kids would think to do back in the

'80s, when not everyone had a home computer, and forget about an Internet connection, I went to my local library and looked up the terrain of the camp area on a computer.

I found orienteering maps with details about where to find the hills, open land, forests and streams. I looked up what kind of vegetation there was, and what plants and berries might be edible. I found out what the fishing was like, and what the best spots for catching them might be along Broad Creek.

Now I'm not an outdoorsy kind of guy. My father, Jerome Fennoy, will tell you that as a small boy I used to hate going on our family camping trips to the Smoky Mountains. I don't like getting dirty and I don't like bugs. But I figured the more I planned, the less I would have to suffer the many inconveniences of nature.

I found a spot for us to set up camp just a few kilometers off a hiking trail. It was by a creek, where I knew there was trout we could catch for our dinner. There was a raised piece of open land near a rock face and the edge of a forest. We'd be able to build a shelter in case it rained that night, and we would be able to make a fire from what we found on the forest floor. The raised ground would keep us dry, and the rock face would protect us from wind.

Needless to say I earned that merit badge. But I also learned something that would stay with me throughout my career: planning gives you the edge!

I ditched the brown shorts by the time I joined Numarx at sixteen. Somehow the two things didn't seem to go together, and I was sick of the teasing from my homeboys. But even though I was in a rap group, I never stopped being a Boy Scout. My penchant for planning earned me the nickname I told you about in the first chapter—Krhyme Genius.

When we suspected our road manager was ripping us off, the group turned to me to plot a way to challenge him and catch him in the act. So when we went on tour the next time, I found out from the Baltimore radio station that was sponsoring our performances exactly how much had been budgeted for us. It was $5,000.

On the road I kept copies of all the receipts. In the back of the bus I drew up a ledger and added up all the expenses with the calculator I'd brought along with me. Pretty soon we'd gathered enough evidence to prove our manager was putting the squeeze on us. When we pulled into McDonald's and he told us we could only have McNuggets and some tap water to stay under budget, we knew it was time for a showdown.

He said, "Look, hotels cost money. I'm putting you up in the Holiday Inn. I think you'll agree it's a fine hotel. They even shine your shoes!"

I said, "Hold up, how much is the nightly rate?"

When he told me it was $250 a room I knew he was full of it. Right in front of him I went to a pay phone and called the hotel reservation desk. The rack rate was just $75 a night. We let him have it. I showed him the receipts. We were halfway through the trip and, by my calculation, we still had more than $4,000 in our travel budget.

We told him that if he didn't start spending the money and taking care of us like he was supposed to, we'd put the word out that he was scamming the radio station and pocketing the cash for himself. There we were, four sixteen-year-old boys staring down a grown man with all his experience in the music industry. But doing the homework gave us the courage. When we confronted him he had to capitulate, because I was prepared. That night we ate steak and lobster.

I won't go to a meeting without preparing for it. Every day we get a report that tells us exactly how many spins a particular single got at a radio station. The numbers are prepared and bound in a file for me. By 9:00 a.m., before everyone else is sitting at their desks, I've already read through the numbers and mentally downloaded their meaning.

If I'm meeting someone, I do a search about that person on the Internet so I know where his or her head is at. You don't sit across from the dinner table from somebody like Larry Probst, CEO of Electronic Arts, the biggest video-game publisher in the world, without knowing what his latest products in development are, or how his sales are doing. You make it your business to know about their business!

Coming up at Def Jam demanded a lot of preparation. It was my job to get artists to their destinations on time. If they didn't make it to their interviews, if they blew off performances or appearances at awards shows or specials, they'd not only hurt our sales and damage our relationships with the media outlets, they'd disappoint their fans and damage their careers.

So I was a stickler for running through the details beforehand. If I had to be in North Fork, Virginia, by 8:00 a.m. one morning and I didn't know the route, I'd leave the night before to make sure I didn't run into any traffic problems or detours. I might arrive dead-ass tired, but at least I'd be on time.

I prided myself on getting the logistics just right. When Def Jam started hiring people to work under me, I tried to instill the same kind of forward thinking into the people I was training up. But I didn't always succeed.

Back in 1996 when I was the national promotions manager, working on building our West Coast operation, we hired a guy to go on a concert tour with me. It was his job to do the driving, make sure the car was working and figure out where we were going. I was overseeing the welfare of the artists and dealing with the various concert venues we'd be performing at along the way.

It was a grueling tour. Over fourteen days we drove from Seattle to Denver, to Phoenix, to San Diego and then back to L.A. I told my guy over and over again to always make sure the car was gassed up the night before. He said, "Yeah, yeah, I'm on it." I figured okay, he's on it, I don't have keep repeating myself.

After the last concert, we spent the night in San Diego. Then we got up early the next day to take the artist home. Suddenly I noticed that the needle on the fuel gauge had sunk to the bottom. We were out of gas in the middle of a freeway in South Central L.A.!

Luckily, we were near an off-ramp going down hill. We gunned the engine to build up some speed from the fumes that were left, and when the engine cut out I jumped out of the car and pushed us to the nearest gas station.

It was appalling to me. Breaking down in the middle of a freeway with an artist was right up there on my list of worst mess-ups. But Mellow, the artist who was in the car with us at the time, was just enjoying the show. He was laughing so hard, watching me, the Def Jam boss, huffing and puffing on a California highway, that we were able to make a joke out of the situation. We were lucky Mellow was one of the most mellow rap artists I've ever dealt with.

Needless to say, that representative didn't last much longer at Def Jam.

Think Before You Act

There's nothing wrong with going by your gut. But like the old African proverb says, "Only a fool tests to see how deep the water is with both feet."

The best person I know for thinking things through is Jay-Z. Even though he's an artist who uses emotion to express himself, he takes a calculating, businesslike approach to every decision he makes. Jay never does anything without going back and forth a few times, canvassing the judgments of people he trusts and weighing the pros and cons. Like me, he routinely draws up a list of the positives and negatives to help him decide.

The other day I asked him about how his mind works. This is what he told me:

"At the end of the day, this is a business, and emotional decisions are not good for business. I have been able, through God's grace, to step outside of my body and ask myself: 'What does Jay-Z the artist need to do? What do I, Shawn Carter, need to do? Is this about the business or the BS?' "

Jay has never been easily swayed by the opinions of others. After the whole drawn-out process of analysis, he usually ends up going with an instinct that flies in the face of everybody's advice but turns out to be a brilliant career move. He lines up his head with his heart, then he acts.

He made his *Blueprint* album, a deeply personal and emotional statement, just when his career was peaking. Anyone else's logic would dictate that he cut some vinyl people could dance to in the clubs to capitalize on the momentum of success, but his decision to do the opposite took him to the next level as an artist and he *still* had multiplatinum sales.

Not many people would have made the decision to retire at the height of their success. But last year, at the age of thirty-four, Jay decided he would go out with a bang and produce the *Black Album*, which would be his last. He was taking the biggest risk of his music career.

The work had to be his best yet. But it also had to be his final expression as a rap artist, and a statement to his fans about why he was choosing to step back. Through his art, he had to find a way to make his transition from Jay-Z back to Shawn Carter; from rap artist to entrepreneur.

He went way out on a limb with his "99 Problems" video. He took a risk that the censors would go crazy with the violence and religious references. I had to personally go to the program directors of all the video stations, MTV and BET, to fight for his right to air the video intact. They kept telling Julie Greenwald and me no, but Jay wouldn't compromise. He refused to allow his art to be censored.

There was nothing gratuitous about "99 Problems." Everything in it was there for a reason. The references to racial profiling, the struggle against poverty and the trappings of wealth and fame summed up the themes of his rhyming over a decade. The scene where Jay gets shot up, with his hands up in a gesture of a crucifixion, was to show how the old Jay-Z was dying and making way for Shawn.

His strategy hit the mother lode. Not only did he produce a great swan song and one of the greatest achievements of his career to date, Jay sold millions of albums and won numerous awards, including a Grammy. Months after he announced his retirement in 2004 he was still the hottest-selling rap artist. With more than 20 million in album sales over the span of his music-making career, a partnership in Roc-A-Fella (a $500 million empire) and projects in filmmaking, sellout tours and dozens of artistic collaborations as a producer, Jay has laid the foundation for the next chapter: stepping into my world as the next president and CEO of Def Jam.

Like he told me, "I always wanted to be a boss."

I wish him the best of luck.

Don't Get Stuck in the Paralysis of Analysis

Sometimes people get into a mode where they are planning so much that they never make a decision. All that weighing up of pros and cons needs to lead somewhere. You have to act, because if you spend too long on the cyphering, someone else is going to come along and steal your position.

Be like Jay. Size up the situation. Be the cool-headed cat,

then pounce. There is no reward without a certain amount of risk. Just make sure you have a Plan B and a built-in ability to make the necessary adjustments along the way.

Some of the greatest success stories in business have been a combination of risk measuring and risk taking. No one believed in the possibility of a twenty-four-hour cable news channel before Ted Turner surveyed the market and then leapt into the gaping hole to create CNN.

In the 1980s, *The Bill Cosby Show* was repeatedly turned down by ABC and CBS. NBC finally took a risk, but they knew the material was good and that American viewing audiences were ready for a sitcom about a middle-class black family with a positive message. No one knew for sure if it was going to succeed. It had been passed over numerous times by other people in the industry. But it became one of the highest-rated prime time shows of all time and elevated NBC to the top of the three main television networks.

Everything about the business I'm in is based on calculated risk. Music is one of the most subjective products you can sell. We pour hundreds of thousands of dollars into our rap artists with no guarantee that they're going to go platinum or even gold. The best we can do is sign stars, set high standards in the studio and do the groundwork to make sure a fickle market is hot for the new joints we put out.

In 1980, Bob Johnson, the CEO of Black Entertainment Television, or BET, took a huge risk starting a music video channel with black music content. The prevailing wisdom at the time was that no one would watch it. It was hard to get any black artists played on MTV when it began soon after in 1981. But today BET is one of the leading black-owned and -operated entertainment companies in the world, creating hundreds of jobs for African-Americans who might not otherwise find opportunities in television.

Bob did his market research and managed to convince himself and his investors that there was a reasonable likelihood of success. But, like he says, "risk is part of the terrain."

Researching the reward, then taking the risk, helped BET continue to grow. Four years ago, a junior employee in his programming department came up with the idea to move production to New York, after BET had already invested millions of dollars in facilities and equipment in D.C. But New York is where all the talent is.

They came up with the idea for *106 & Park*, which became the top-rated video show in the country. All the best recording artists and movie stars in the country stop by the studio, conveniently located in midtown Manhattan.

Too often people within a company get stuck in "group think." They plan, but they're never comfortable enough to say, "Okay, we've looked at it in every way possible, now it's time to take action." They're afraid to stick their neck out for fear of getting shot down.

But having boldness of thought is a great way to get noticed. If it's a company with a healthy culture that appreciates innovative ideas, you could be tapped to be the next. Even if you're just a small cog in the wheel of an organization, never be afraid to act aggressively on a well-researched idea that you believe in. The employee who suggested the move to the Big Apple is now one of BET's top executives.

Embrace Change

Never let your faith in a plan allow you to miss the opportunity of a changing situation.

When I stood outside my high school auditorium on graduation day and told my mother I wanted to make $30,000 as an engineer so that I could afford to shop at a store like Macy's, who knew I'd end up as president of Def Jam? I'm glad I didn't stick to that plan!

It's telling to me how some people react to change.

When I had to let go of my old assistant, Tracey Smith, she was so cool with it that we were out having drinks with our mutual friends, Rod and Tuffy, that same night.

"Yo Tracey, do you have to look so happy?" I asked her.

"Kevin, you know how I like to keep it movin'," she replied.

A homegirl from back in Baltimore, Tracey recognized that she just wasn't personal assistant material. She came to New York to work closely with me and see how a major record company operates from the inside. But she wasn't so crazy about all the little administrative details she had to take care of. By the time we had the conversation about what she was going to do next, she already got what she needed from her gig with me: insight and contacts.

Tracey has always had that entrepreneurial spirit. She had offers to be on staff at other record labels. But she knew herself well enough to realize she'd be better off as a free agent. Today she's a manager for Comp, a hot new artist. No doubt she's got several other hustles going on in the music world.

I know Shante Bacon is destined for success because she figured out when it was the right time to go. Shante joined Def Jam in 1998, before it was sold to Vivendi Universal and was still a small, entrepreneurial operation on Varick Street. She dreamed about working at the company she was in love with since she was 11. "I am a hip-hop girl," she'd tell me.

But what she was *not* was the corporate type. Moving to the big office tower in midtown Manhattan was the end of an era for Shante. We were still a family at Def Jam, but we had to adapt to a new structure and operate in an organization with hundreds of other employees. The flavor changed and it wasn't possible to have daily contact and deep discussions with everyone in every department. Little things like cranking up the music really loud or burning incense at her desk had to stop. It took her well over a year to adjust.

"I was totally opposed to change," says Shante today. "I'd always ask, 'Why isn't it like so and so?' But I'm learning that you can learn a lot more from situations when you're not in your comfort zone."

After six years and four promotions, Shante began to realize that she couldn't rise any higher at Def Jam. She wasn't excited to come to work anymore and felt sick in her soul. So, in July 2004, she left.

Today, she's senior director of marketing at SoBe, a Warner start-up label based out of Miami. With just ten employees, she gets into every aspect of running a record label, from getting videos played to getting artists promoted in print publications. She's happy because she's learning the business in a whole new way and building the experience she needs to start her own label someday. I wish her the best of luck.

When you first veer off the path you've mapped out for yourself, it can seem like a disaster. It scares me. Sometimes I fight like hell to get back on course. But sometimes it's better to embrace the change.

"Know when to go," says Shante. "Don't just hang on to it and hope it's going to get better."

The most momentous and beneficial changes in my life were forced on me. It was only years later that I came to realize how fate was actually sending me in the direction I needed to go all along.

When I was kicked off my high school football team because I made the choice to pursue my music career, I was crushed, but it freed me up to concentrate on what I had to do. When my grades were so bad in college that I lost my scholarship, it propelled me to make the drastic decision of dropping out, but that was one more event in my life that enabled me to focus the career path I was meant to follow.

The toughest change forced on me early on in my career was when I left World Connections Travel. I'd worked there from the ages of seventeen to twenty-two. My boss, Jim Buckingham, a young white guy not much older than me, had become my mentor. By the time I left I was earning $50,000 a year, which was a fortune to me and my family at the time. My mother had to work for a decade as an accountant before she could bring home $40,000 a year.

But the time had come for me to step up full-blown for Def Jam. The label finally offered me a paid position to run regional promotions. I had to be on call 24/7 for them. At a moment's notice I might have had to fly across the country. I couldn't keep my commitment to the other job, so I was forced to make a sacrifice. Def Jam was my destiny.

The powers at Def Jam needed me to show the love. All that time I'd been grinding for them as an intern, I was still living at home, running various schemes from my parents' basement. I was close to my mother and father and I liked being around my baby sisters. I'd never lived away from home. I never really even thought about leaving. It was too easy and comfortable to stay right where I was.

A few weeks after I accepted the full-time position, Wes "Party" Johnson, the vice president of promotions and my new boss at Def Jam, pulled up outside the door of our house in Baltimore in his shiny black limo. Wes decided to take me to L.A., where I'd be working under his wing out of Le Montrose, a luxury hotel in Hollywood, to help build up the West Coast office. I'd be out there for the next three months.

My mother couldn't stop bawling. She still cries about it to this day. Here was this big, slick dude with a booming voice she'd never met before coming to take her baby boy away. She knew I'd be living the life in five-star hotels, having my laundry done for me and eating in the best restaurants. She knew there was no way I was ever coming back to Baltimore to live. So did Wes, Russell and Lyor.

Keep it Moving

After fifteen years at Def Jam, I had to face another major change that wasn't part of my plan. On July 6, 2004, Antonio "L.A." Reid—the man brought in by Universal Music Group to be our new CEO—relieved me of my duties. Looking back on the past year, I can see it was meant to be.

For months I'd been feeling confused about where I stood at Def Jam and within the Universal Music Group. I couldn't get a clear picture of where the company was headed. That feeling of unease started seeping under my skin long before some of the changes went down. Over the years there's been a lot of restructuring, merging and demerging. The industry was taking a beating with the recession and digital downloading. The mood was getting sour.

The previous New Year's I went to Anguilla. It should have been a blast. There I was, staying in a beautiful six-room villa overlooking the sea, chilling in a Caribbean paradise complete with a butler and the best luxuries life has to offer, and feeling like my life wasn't complete. My equilibrium was thrown off. I didn't feel whole.

I rarely have moments like that in life. I'm usually so busy I don't have that much time to think. But when it hits me, I pay attention to it. I make a mental list of all of the most important things in my life, and I take stock. Then I break it down.

Every morning I got up just after sunrise to go alone to a cliff-top and peer down into the water. It helped me to clear my head and think. I looked at five things: my spirit, my finances, my relationship, my family and my career. My family was straight; I have beautiful kids. In the way of material things, I couldn't ask for more. I have the houses, the cars, etc. I was happy with what I'd achieved, but knew there was a distance yet for me to go.

I looked across the sea to St. Martin, an eight-minute flight away. "Damn," I thought to myself. "If success is the distance between Anguilla and St. Martin, then I am only eight minutes away. How am I going to get there?"

Financially I was already successful, at least compared with 98 percent of America. I'm almost there spiritually as well. But I had to wonder, "Have I consumed enough of a certain thing that I can move on mentally to the next thing. Am I happy with what I've accomplished in music?" I'm no Clive Davis. I'm no Berry Gordy. I still have a long way to go to satisfy myself mentally.

Then I got a call from Edgar Bronfman Jr. It just so happened that Edgar had a house nearby, and was staying in Anguilla over the holidays with his wife and children.

Edgar wanted me to come over for lunch, meet his family and get to know him. We'd already met, when Edgar ran Universal, but we hadn't had much contact in those days. He'd seen me in the building and he knew my reputation, but he was curious about Kevin the person. So I stopped by in the afternoon and we sat on his terrace and talked for hours about our lives, our beliefs, our hopes and ambitions. Before I knew it the sun was setting over the sea and we'd become friends.

The meeting couldn't have come at a better time. Edgar made it clear he wanted me on board at Warner Music Group. But what struck me about this man was how he related to me on a human level. I was going through a divorce at the time, and he'd been through one himself, so he wanted to make sure I was all right.

I left his villa that night feeling like somebody took notice. My whole career I'd been with Lyor and Russell and we were like family, but recognition from Edgar made me lift up my head and realize that I was also valued outside the Def Jam building. I wasn't ready to leave the label at that point, but I filed that meeting in the back of my head and promised myself I'd stay in touch with Edgar.

Soon after I got back to New York, my boss and mentor Lyor Cohen left to go to Warner. Instead of promoting me to CEO, the Universal executives brought in L.A., who'd just been made available when he was asked to leave another record label, Arista.

For most of my adult life, I had a house called Def Jam. The guy who helped me build the house left. The bank that financed the house, Universal, said they weren't sure if I could still manage the house on my own. They thought that, at thirty-five, I was too young to be CEO. I was also perceived as Lyor's guy. They feared I might give away trade secrets to the competition.

That wasn't true of course. I looked at it with the same mindset as any football player whose friend gets recruited to another team. In the business world, just like in the NFL, when you get drafted you've got to be loyal to the team, but you can still be great friends.

The company's decision left me feeling confused. I would rather not do anything than be confused. I started saying to myself, "Damn, the check is good, but am I going to be happy?" Then I started thinking, "Well, the check ain't good enough so screw this, I can be happy." I resigned, just days before one of the biggest awards shows in the music industry: the Grammys.

My decision shocked everyone. But I felt great! I was still working for Def Jam. I gave them three weeks' notice. As soon as word spread, I was getting all kinds of calls, from executives at Sony and American Express wanting to offer me a job to people in the industry asking me if I could take them wherever I was going.

The next day I flew to Los Angeles. At the Grammy Awards that week I was the talk of the town. I wanted to wear a T-shirt emblazoned with the words "Free Agent." People came up to me and said, "Kev, you're the hottest thing since Janet Jackson when she bared her breast at the Super Bowl!"

I felt like the kid who graduates from high school with solid A's and has to choose between going to Harvard, Yale or Princeton. For the first time since I was a teenager I was looking out on an open horizon of options. The whole world was spread in front of me.

Days later, I got a call from Doug Morris, the CEO of Universal. They knew I was the backbone of the company. I was the brand. They offered me a three-year contract worth millions of dollars and equity in the company if I'd stay.

L.A. Reid is good at what he does. He's a brilliant producer. He breaks great artists. He's the man with the platinum ears. In the first half of last year he had six artists in the top ten. His roster of acts swept up their share of Grammys. But he wasn't a hip-hop guy. No one knew if he had the experience in the rap world that Def Jam was built on.

I thought long and hard about it. I was still attached to Def Jam and the people I worked with, and I wanted to take it to a whole new level. Russell convinced me that it could be the next Disney. He wanted me to stay to continue to build up the brand.

The prospect of working with L.A. started to appeal to me. We could set an example: two African-American men running their own top record label. He was the creative guy; I was the operations guy with the street edge. There could be a clear delineation of what we did for the company. He could be a good ying to my yang. I accepted the offer and stayed.

But as the weeks passed, the reality of the situation started to sink in. We had a lot of work to do. Our staff needed to get fired up again. Politics had crept in like a cancer, dividing everyone. It wasn't as much fun to get out of bed and go to work anymore. I was still working longer and harder than everybody else, but I felt like I was wearing golden handcuffs.

Then in March L.A. called me into his office. He wanted to know if I was sure I wanted to be there. He took me aside and said, "You know, you gave me the keys to the house and said, 'Oh well,' but I expected you to show me every room."

I told him that I was committed and I wouldn't have come back if I wasn't sure. I said, "L.A., if we're going to try and make it work, let's try and make it work."

L.A. thanked me for the conversation, and I continued to do my job. As always, Def Jam employees made a beeline to my office, not L.A.'s. It was natural. People knew me, and they were comfortable with me. I'd been there for a long time, and they knew I knew how to deal with the artists. My door was always open.

L.A.'s style was different. He liked people to call him Mr. Reid. He ran a tight ship, and introduced more formality at his end of the hallway. There's nothing wrong with that, but it took some getting used to for those more familiar with the Def Jam Way.

I knew it would be hard at first, but I thought we were all finally starting to vibe together. I was getting rid of people who I could tell were dividing the organization and playing politics, and we seemed to have the personnel changes we needed in place to make it work. I figured wrong.

On the Monday after Fourth of July weekend, 2004, I left the building and never went back. It was a shock. Def Jam had been my life for fifteen years. I'd already been through the emotional turmoil of leaving and coming back again. But I knew it was the right thing to do.

We tried to make it work, L.A. and I, but our management styles were just not compatible. If I can't make it work, it's time to move on.

I don't blame L.A. It is what it is. In a way, it was inevitable. You can't have two big and very different personalities at the helm of a business culture and expect it to work. It was the decision he felt he had to make to take total control. The fact that I had resigned a few months earlier, and the elation I felt back then at the prospect of the unknown, were already signs that this change was meant to be.

That doesn't mean it was easy. For a week I sat by my pool in Warren, New Jersey, trying to separate myself and absorb what happened. I was anxious and sad. It wasn't so much that I was worried about getting another job. I knew I'd find something equal to, or greater than, the job I'd just left. But Def Jam had been my life for a decade and a half. I lived, breathed and bled that company. I felt I was Def Jam. In many ways, the label had become my identity.

No one else could believe it. When Russell found out, he said, "Kev, what the f___, what the f___?" Jay-Z whisked me off in his private jet a day later so that we could hang out at his video set in Los Angeles. All the way there he kept echoing Russell: "What the f___, Kev? What the f___?" The first few days after it went down it felt like I was spending most of my time consoling other people!

A few weeks later, L.A. checked in to see if I was okay and ask whether I'd found a new position to my liking. This is what I wrote to him:

Hey man, it looks like things are progressing. It's hard for me to say anything is done, until I see it in black and white.

I wanted to express to you how hard this process has been for my family, my friends (a lot of them under your watch) and most of all myself.

My family: For the past 15 years, I've done nothing but build, protect and serve a brand that is now recognized throughout the world. I served in the most loyal and honest ways I know how. Waking up every morning while my kids were still asleep and returning after they were already in bed. Sacrificing family for the sake of an ad on radio, a new artist's signing, more **BDS** spins etc. . . . Missing the very first steps of both of my children. I knew the choice I was making and I was ready for the consequences of my actions.

My first family became Def Jam. Whether wrong or right, I stand by that decision 'til this very day. From every assistant, intern, manager, director, I pledged my love and life for their success and well being. Knowing this you can truly understand my parents', sisters' and brother's shock when the news broke that I would no longer be at the brand I wore so proudly on my chest. My mom came to me crying, praying and hoping that I would be okay. Not because her son was unemployed, but because she knew what the brand meant to me. I've spent the last couple weeks putting family first and trying to convince them that I will be okay.

My friends: I never just worked with my co-workers at the company. We actually all grew up together. Our successes and failures molding the very character and integrity that we embody today. I feel my five- to 15-year relationship with each of them was put on trial to see where their loyalty stood, when all I ever wanted was to provide access and opportunity for each of them. They all deserve the best IDJ [Island Def Jam Music Group] has to give and I ask you personally to see that they are afforded every opportunity to prosper and grow.

Myself: I am preparing myself for the next phase of my career. Closing the last chapter on a book that I not only co-wrote, but also published. I can't tell you how focused this experience has made me. We all have to make decisions that we have to learn to live with. The greatest thing is that we all have choices. I'm in great spirits and could only wish you the best.

Strangely enough, I'm glad it happened the way it did. Getting that push forced me to think about what was good for Kevin and Kevin only. I was much more than the brand I'd built up for so many years, and I was finally ready to accept that. Moving forward without Def Jam Records was not part of my plan, but it felt right. It's freed me up to move on to the next phase of my career as executive vice president of Warner Music Group.

The Next

Was it fate that I happened to have a lunch meeting with Edgar Bronfman over at Warner the very same day I found out I was leaving Def Jam? I like to think so. I'd only set it up a few weeks before to network, but Edgar had other ideas. I'd entertained various offers in the weeks that followed, but I kind of knew I'd go with WMG. It was Edgar's spirit, and the human interest he took in my well-being, that tipped the scales. Not many top executives in this cutthroat industry start off their conversations with each other by asking sincere questions about how they're doing on a personal level.

A couple of days later I flew to Los Angeles with Jay-Z to keep him company while he was filming MTV's first "mash-up" with

Linkin Park. No contracts had been signed, but everyone seemed to know I was done at Def Jam and going over to Warner, which happens to own the label that Linkin Park is on. Soon I would be responsible for that group's welfare.

That night we all got together for dinner at Tom Whalley's house in Beverly Hills. Tom is the chairman of Warner Bros. Records based in the West Coast, so he was about to become my colleague within the Warner Music Group. Tom, me, Jay and the guys in Linkin Park spent the evening vibing together. I instantly assumed my role as caretaker for all the artists and put everybody at ease.

There I was with my old friend Jay, coming out of my life at a hip-hop label and meeting hot new artists of a different genre. I was able to be the bridge between their two worlds. It was a great moment. I realized then that all the turbulence in my life over the past few days had happened for a reason.

But the hard work of adjusting to a new job hadn't even begun. I spent the rest of the summer vacationing with Jay and his girlfriend Beyoncé in Capri, Monte Carlo and Nice, so it wasn't until the day after Labor Day that I actually set foot in my new office.

It was overwhelming. Day one I was in back-to-back meetings. I must have met dozens of new people as groups of three or four executives at a time from the different labels in our group trudged into the conference room to discuss the nuts and bolts of our various businesses. First we had the blueprint meeting, where we discussed the overall direction and priorities of Warner Music Group. We discussed what the next two quarters were going to look like for the business as a whole, and which artists would be our primary focus, and in which markets. Then we had budget meeting after budget meeting as we discussed the financial health of our labels: Atlantic, Lava, Maverick, Nonesuch, Reprise, Rhino, Sire, Asylum, Warner Bros. and Word.

We had a conference via satellite with our colleagues all over the world for Warner Music International. I also met the executives at Warner Strategic Marketing, Alternative Distribution, and Warner/Chappell, one of the leading music publishers in the world.

It struck me that I was dealing with a very different beast from Def Jam. Back there, I was in charge of one brand, housed in a single building, not some multi-faceted, billion-dollar conglomerate with operations all over the world. At Def Jam, I was able to know the intricate details of one label from the ground up. I knew the habits, ambitions, strengths and weaknesses of every employee. I was involved in hiring 80 percent of them. I'm used to knowing everyone else's schedule and being hands-on, down to the way the receptionist answers the phone. But here, at Warner, I had to know what makes each company tick a dozen times over, and put it in the context of the big picture. At Def Jam, I was one of the label executives coming to report. Here at Warner I was sitting in a conference room looking at the whole scope. By the end of that first budget meeting, I had a headache!

But I didn't try to take in every detail all at once. Neil Craven, an executive in Warner's finance department, said, "Kevin, don't try to remember every single thing you hear today. Just catch the buzzwords and numbers, and I'll brief you on the rest later."

That was good advice. I took notes and paid attention to the people in those meetings, then Neil broke each meeting down for me in one-paragraph summaries that delivered the essentials. I'm so glad he did that. I realized that day that this process of learning a new company would take time and a lot of shorthand!

That's true of any new gig. Don't try to download all at once. You'll just get frustrated. Sketch it out for yourself and color in the rest of the details later. The key is to learn where you fit in the big picture, and which people on your team can help you draw it all together.

The next few weeks I set about getting the feel of the place. It was quiet in the head office. There was a much more traditional corporate feel to the environment at Warner. My office suite on the top floor made me feel a little isolated, and I couldn't exactly walk the floors when our companies were so spread out, so I had to figure out some other ways to get to know my new colleagues. I discovered which elevator bay at 75 Rockefeller adjoined our head office with our marketing company, and made a point of chatting with the key folks who I happened to bump into at that intersection when I was between appointments. I set up lunches, dinners, breakfasts and coffee meetings with employees and counterparts almost every day for the next several weeks.

That was essential. All the restructuring at WMG took place before I came, and everyone was in place, each playing their own positions. I wasn't coming in to fire existing staff and hire new people like I did at Def Jam. These guys were already running their business units and making money for the company. They were set in their ways, and it was my job to find out what those ways were.

All in all, it's been a humbling experience. Wherever you move on to next, you have to accept that you'll be climbing a steep learning curve, no matter what your position. But I was ready. Everything I'd done in my life has prepared me for this latest phase in my career. Over the past few years I've made a point of networking with leaders from all walks of business life. When I was expanding the brand for Def Jam I vibed with executives from Wal-Mart, Electronic Arts and American Greetings. Hanging out with billionaires like Edgar Bronfman, Bob Johnson and Jamaican-born fund manager Michael Lee-Chin has given me the opportunity to watch them up close and learn how they wheel and deal.

I helped build two companies with Russell and Lyor. Now I'm part of a team that bought a company and is in the process of rebuilding it. We've gone public with the most talked-about IPO of the year and I own a piece of it. It may not be the traditional destination for hip hop, but here I am at the helm of an organization where I can effect change in the music and publishing industries and garner new respect for our culture. These are things I can add to my resume.

Whatever comes next, BRING IT ON!

 RULE 4

What: Create a Blueprint

Why: You'll need a road map to success. Create a vision to help you see where it all fits. Focusing on the big picture will help you edit out the things that distract you from success.

How: Make planning part of the way you live your life. Prepare, research and focus on the task in front of you. Be alert and present at all times.

But: Allow room for change. Don't limit yourself to one path. The surprises along the way could be even better than what's on the blueprint.

Rule 5

Play Your Position

Do what must be done.

—Jim Collins, *Good to Great*

No job is beneath you.

If someone asks you to do something that you think is too menial, don't take offense. There are no shortcuts when you're starting out in business. Success in any career you choose requires a sense of humility and a desire to start at the beginning.

Houses get built from the ground up. All the real work gets done at the bottom end of an organization. You can't run a business unless someone answers the phone. You can't pitch a marketing plan unless someone is there to type it up. You can't promote a concert without some kid to hand out the flyers.

There's a myth out there that the success stories of hip hop just somehow glided to the top. Kids actually believe the Russells and Sean Combses of this world made it there by acting cool and pumping up the attitude. I've lost count of the number of times someone starts out as my assistant and, a year later, expects to be promoted to director or vice president. That's crazy to me!

P. Diddy had to start somewhere. At Uptown Records, he worked as an intern. He made photocopies, ran errands and fetched lunch. He never complained. He just made sure he did it right. Puffy might be living the life now, but people don't see the grinding that goes on behind the scenes to get to that point.

You have to play your present position, whatever it is, to the best of your ability, no matter how low you are on the totem pole. But that doesn't mean you have to limit yourself to one job. Look around your environment to see if there is a task you can perform outside of your immediate realm of responsibility. No one expects you to stay locked inside a box. But they aren't going to see what you're worth until you've shown them.

This reminds me of another one of my former employees, Amber Noble. The first time I met Amber was several years ago at the Impact Music Conference in Miami. She was a smart, young promotion and marketing director at Radio One Station, WPHZ, in Philadelphia. Back then she was working ten hours a day while simultaneously attending Temple University. Amber made it her business to introduce herself to me and hand me her business card. She was always very respectful of my time and the environment in which we met. She always played her position.

As chance would have it, Amber sent me a page one evening. A reminder that she was ready. I have to admit it, many of her pages would go unreturned and others would receive a brief courtesy reply. But on this particular message, Amber wrote something like, "You know I'm Def. I like to Jam and you know I got Soul." It was the corniest thing in the world, but I have to give her credit for having the guts to write it. As fate would have it, an executive assistant position became available, and she was the person I thought of.

I returned Amber's page at around 7:00 a.m. the following morning and explained to her that I had a job available, so she should call my office. She was extremely eager and called my office as soon as I hit the door and was on the first train smoking.

She offered me a copy of her resume. I didn't need it and immediately offered her the job as my new executive assistant. I knew it was a tough adjustment to go from a bigger title (by the radio industry's standards) to being an assistant. However, it was clear that Amber knew what she wanted and was willing to make the sacrifice.

For more than two years, Amber played her position as my assistant. No task was too small or too big. A title never defined Amber. Instead, her hard work and commitment to the team made her an asset to our organization. Amber is now the senior director of marketing at Def Jam.

If you're the receptionist, you can do other things besides answering the phone. If you work in the mailroom in a music company, for example, you can still branch out and learn about promotions. Most employers respect and encourage their employees' efforts to stretch themselves. The trick is to have your own backyard covered. Be a specialist before you become a generalist.

Don't make the mistake of clinging to your position, though. Understand the difference between marking your territory and being territorial. You mark your territory by covering your base so well that no one else can compete. That's a good thing. But being territorial is a sign of insecurity. When people are overprotective of their positions, it's a sign they feel threatened by others on the team. They see their colleagues as rivals and try to keep them down.

Take ownership, but team ownership. It's what's ours, not what's mine. If you internalize it and make it all about you, you become territorial and you can't win, not in the long term.

Play your position so well that everybody wins.

Play for the Team

Swallow your pride. The job isn't about you, it's about the cause. When the whole organization does well, it'll lift you higher than you could ever go on your own. Before you can be a superstar, you have to learn to be a great team player.

Roll your sleeves up, put your head down and think about how your work can best serve others in doing their job. Even Derek Jeter plays his position. He exercises with the team. He shows up for spring training. Beyoncé shows up on time, every day. When she has a show, she puts in hours rehearsing with her dancers, band members and stage hands.

Stop playing for the team and you start losing the game. Dallas Cowboy safety Roy Williams has a word for those ego players who think they're too high and mighty to play their position: cancer.

"You've got to have a strong core," he says. "You've got to have all eleven players on the field with you and know that everyone has each other's back. Once somebody on the field thinks they're so great they can do whatever they want, other members of the team lose their groove. They don't know how to play it or who to pass the ball to; they stop trusting each other. You've got Bob telling you to go right and Bill telling you to go left, then suddenly you're all over the place. You don't know what to believe. Everybody's steering you in the wrong direction."

If he ever decided to retire from the NFL, I'd hire Roy. He's learned about life and success from one of the best schools out there: team sports. That's where you learn what it really means to be part of a group of individuals who are all working toward a goal that is bigger than themselves. In football, if you play your position on defense, no one can score on you.

Don't be a cancer. Play for the team.

No Job Is Too Small

There's nothing wrong with a winning attitude. Ambition is necessary to make it happen. But don't have an unchecked ego. Don't let foolish pride trick you into mistaking opportunities for insults. No job is too small. If it helps you to get even one inch closer to where you need to go, accept it with good grace.

Even Edgar Bronfman Jr., heir to the vast Seagram fortune, had to prove himself in a job he called "chief schlepper" at his family business. His dad wasn't just going to start him at the top. Edgar had to show his humility and willingness to put his head down by answering the phone, taking messages, delivering the interoffice mail, making coffee and copying documents.

Back in the day, I was like any other kid with a big dream and a big head to match. At nineteen, when we got our first royalty check for "Girl You Know It's True," I blew a few thousand dollars on one of the first cell phones. That thing was the size of a shoebox!

We were in Los Angeles for the BMI Awards at the time. BMI is a performing rights organization that represents songwriters and composers. We'd won an award for best song, so we decided to go out to Venice Beach and party the next day. We took a few pictures as I posed with my new cell phone. I still have that picture. There I was, wading in the surf with my pants rolled up and this beast of a phone strapped to my shoulder, a music mogul in the making!

By the time I went for a job at the mighty Def Jam in 1991, I figured they'd be lucky to have me. My band, Numarx, was the hot ticket in Baltimore. All over the mid-Atlantic area we were opening for acts like Run DMC, Salt-N-Pepa and LL Cool J. Our songs were getting played on the radio, even on New York City stations. I'd made that hit.

My band and I founded our own record label, Marx Bros. We

were pressing our own vinyl and producing records for other bands. I was working on street teams on behalf of major record labels, getting spins at radio stations and letting people know when a major act was coming to town.

I knew everyone there was to know in music, radio and clubs in the greater metropolitan area of Baltimore and D.C. Hell, I was a local celebrity! I thought Def Jam should be knocking at my door. I could get any of their records played and sold!

Then I heard about the "Jack the Rapper" conference in Atlanta. It was one of the first summits for hip-hop artists ever. I knew representatives from Def Jam had to be there. It was *the* label for hip hop. All of the artists I loved listening to—Run DMC, the Beastie Boys, LL Cool J—were associated with Def Jam. This was my big chance to make my dream of working there come true.

Me and my homeboys piled in a truck and drove all night from Baltimore to Atlanta. I had no idea how I was going to get access to the conference. I didn't even know who the hell I was supposed to look for. But as soon as we walked in the convention hall, there was the giant burgundy- and silver-colored Def Jam logo in the middle of the lobby.

Looking back it seems kind of corny, but we were so excited to see it there. I had someone take pictures of Rod and me posing in front of it. While I was standing waiting for my picture to be taken I thought to myself, "Some day, I'm going to be president." It was my sign!

Later that day we found a party for some of the industry people at a nearby hotel. I worked the room and asked people who was there from Def Jam. Some guy pointed across the room and there was Wes "Party" Johnson. A big-ass bear of a man, Wes had the look of someone used to livin' large.

I walked up to him and introduced myself. Once I'd told him my name I figured he'd know the rest. At that time, Wes was senior vice president of promotions and marketing at Def Jam. I knew he'd spent time in the Baltimore region hustling for the company. I assumed he must have at least heard about Numarx and our hit song.

But if he did know, he wasn't giving it up. Wes just gave me a blank stare. When I gave him my pitch and told him what I'd done and what I could bring to Def Jam, he shrugged and said they'd had an opening in Baltimore, but they'd just filled it. If I wanted to, I could intern for that guy, Kevin Mitchell, for free.

I said, "Huh? You want me intern for somebody who doesn't know anything about that market? But I'm an artist. Everybody knows me. I already have all this experience!"

"Take it or leave it," Wes said, and walked away.

I thought about it for two seconds. I figured this was my opportunity, either way. I could choose to swallow my pride and make it work for me, or I could just go on being the big fish in the small pond of Baltimore. Once again, it was time for me to take a leap of faith.

I found Wes again. He wasn't hard to miss, propping up the bar and swilling his favorite drink.

"I'll take it," I said.

Years later I found out Wes knew all along who I was. But he had this thing about smart-ass kids who think they are entitled. He wanted to see if I had the humility to accept an unpaid position. He needed to test me. He had to find out if I had the good grace to perform in a job he knew I was overqualified for.

Get the Job Done and Then Some

As soon as I met my new boss, Kevin Mitchell, I knew he needed me.

When he got to Baltimore, he didn't know anyone. I could have exploited the situation. I could have shown him up and made him look bad. But instead I got my grind on and went out of my way to make the boss look good. Kevin was the one with the staff job. My plan was to help him so that he could get a promotion. Then maybe one day I could have his job.

Pretty soon Kevin came to understand what I could do for him. He'd made an appointment to see Frank Ski, who at the time was Baltimore's king of urban radio, but the guys at the station didn't know Kevin Mitchell and refused to let him up. I said to myself, "Now this is the stuff I'm talking about."

I already knew Frank. We went way back to the days when he was deejaying in the clubs. I'd spend just about every Friday and Saturday night in his studio, bringing him Philly cheesesteak sandwiches to eat and Def Jam albums to play. So when Kevin asked for my help, it was simple.

I went over to the station and called up to the studio. I said, "Frank, I've got a new guy here from Def Jam, why don't you let him come up?" Frank said, "Cool, no problem."

Kevin Mitchell never forgot that. In fact, he was so grateful to me for getting him into the station that in the next weekly conference call with Russell and Wes he said, "I don't care what anyone says, my intern Kevin Liles is better than all of us on the phone. This kid can get us in anywhere!"

I said, "Damn, Kevin, please don't say that, they're all going to hate on me."

Maybe a few people did, but I became the one everybody— including Russell, Wes and Lyor—called when they needed to make something happen in the mid-Atlantic region.

For two more years, I hustled hard. I wrote weekly play reports that were pure poetry. At my job at World Connections Travel, I learned to type fifty words per minute. Every day I got into the habit of entering everything into a computer so I would always know what had been done, and what needed to be followed up on.

I focused all my efforts on Kevin Mitchell's behalf. Anything he needed, I got done, even if I had to spend my own money to be effective. If we needed to fill a venue with 2,000 people, I'd herd them in. If a radio program director needed to hear our latest release, I'd get it to him personally, with Kevin Mitchell's best wishes.

My homeboys didn't understand. Rod said, "Kevin, why are you letting Mitchell get all the credit? You know you're the one running this operation."

It all came to a head one weekend when I got an emergency call from Kevin. There was a club in Norfolk, Virginia, that needed some records. It was a four-and-a-half-hour ride to where that deejay was at, but the man needed some vinyl. I just did what I always do. I delivered.

Rod came with me on the ride to keep me company. He was all excited. He figured when we finally got there we were going to party. But as soon as we delivered, Kevin told us to come right back. We spent the whole night driving.

Rod was pissed. He wanted to wait outside Def Jam's Greenbelt offices and hit Kevin Mitchell with a baseball bat. Literally! I wouldn't let him, of course. I said, "Rod, leave him alone, we're better men for it." I knew that some day my reward would come.

Sure enough it did. Lyor had been checking up on Kevin Mitchell to make sure he was keeping up the relationships with key people at the Baltimore area radio stations. Every few weeks or so he'd call and ask, "Has Kevin been there?" Each time they'd say, "Yes, we've seen Kevin," meaning me.

But one day when Russell called Frank Ski, Frank said, "Wait, which Kevin do you mean? Because I've only been seeing one Kevin, and that's Kevin Liles."

I didn't have to brag. I didn't need to undermine Kevin Mitchell. He got promoted out of the Baltimore market and I was left to run things. To get noticed, all I had to do was play my position and serve my boss to the best of my ability. If you do that, you'll shine no matter where you're at in the food chain.

A few days later I got a call from Wes. It was almost midnight and I was out clubbing with my crew. He said, "Be here in New York tomorrow morning at 7:00 for a job interview."

Know Where the Line Is

Once I got my paid position at Def Jam, I was way down low on the totem pole. As a regional promotions manager, I was about as junior as you can get, next to an assistant or an intern. Even though the mid-Atlantic hip-hop market was the hottest thing going at that time outside of New York, I wasn't up at New York headquarters in Russell's and Lyor's faces, so some might say I was at a political disadvantage.

I didn't care. I just wanted to shine through the work I had to do. It was my job to make sure street teams of kids hustled for our artists to get the word out for an album or concert. I was responsible for making sure the deejays played our artists' songs on the radio and in clubs. Being in Baltimore, the market I knew best, enabled me to do that.

Not everyone in the promotions department was carrying the same load. A lot of people were out partying in the clubs until dawn and rolling in at 11:00 a.m. and noon the next day. They felt they got noticed because they were schmoozing with Russell and Lyor and hanging out with the artists.

When the bosses came to town and I didn't join them at the clubs, people said, "Kevin, you've got to get with the program. This is the music industry. This is how we do business here."

I didn't buy that. I figured if I was the boss, I wouldn't want the people on my team hanging out with me and drinking Cristal all night. If I were in charge, I'd be wondering who's back in the building getting the work done.

Coming up, I always told myself, if the boss asks you to dinner or to play golf, no problem. But never, ever offer to take the boss out. I want my higher-ups to respect me because of the great work I do, not because I can take them to a hot restaurant or club. How am I going to make my superior look great if I'm not sitting at my desk, doing what he's not doing?

No matter how easygoing the office environment at Def Jam appeared to be, I knew there was an invisible line and I made it my business to be on the right side of the border. I'd be friendly, but I'd never tell anyone my business unless it was appropriate to share information to get the job done.

I didn't want to get involved in the hype. I knew I had to think for myself. I'd either operate on my own or in a direct line of communication with the mentor or boss I was working under.

I'd joke around, but I never gossiped. I wasn't in a clique. Back then we were a company of twenty people. Even the assistant knew the chairman on a first-name basis. The kind of negative energy that comes from personal politics could have destroyed the fragile structure of a label that size.

One time, when someone tried to bring me in by dissing our boss, I said, "You know what, someday it might be about you. Just like I won't go against you, I'm not going to go against somebody else, so deal with it."

The only time I wanted to huddle was when the coach was calling the play so we all knew who had to block and who had to run. Once the mission was accomplished, I'd be happy to throw my towel up and have a drink with everybody. But while we were on the field I was all about the business.

Sweat the Small Stuff

My professionalism won me the respect of some key supporters. Thomas Lytle, who was director of national promotions and my immediate boss, used every opportunity to talk me up to Russell. He recognized that I was somebody he could depend on to get a job done. He was key in moving me from an internship to a paid position.

It wasn't always a lovefest for Kevin Liles back then. I was the corny kid in Baltimore. I'd always smile and be pleasant, but I became "that annoying dude with the Cheshire cat grin." Whenever I came into New York headquarters, my co-workers in promotions thought I was trying to show them up with my pie charts, laptop and briefcase. What can I say? This industry is as cutthroat as any business can get. Some people were really gunning for me.

So I protected my position. I kept a meticulous record of everything. If something went down, I knew exactly what happened, who was there and when it happened. My anal-retentive insistence on documenting everything helped me to defend myself when someone in my department who'd been at Def Jam longer than me decided that I didn't handle something right and tried to get me fired.

It happened after three months in my paid position. It was the second regional promotional event that I was responsible for coordinating. An artist I was in charge of in my market missed an interview on a music video show. He'd disappeared to smoke some weed and hang out with his friends.

Several people were involved in taking him to where he needed to be. I was putting out some other fire while one of the girls let him slip away from the restaurant where everybody was having lunch. It was on my watch, so I was ultimately responsible. But I was also in charge of running promotions for seven other artists in my market. My time was limited for each one.

So much craziness goes down when you're on a tour. One time, on the *Survival of the Illest* tour, some genius thought it would be funny to leave the bus in neutral while it was parked on a decline. It careened out of control and crashed into a brownstone. At a Run DMC concert in France, crazed fans poured gasoline on the artists' bus and torched it. In this business, you have to document everything just to protect yourself.

When I was questioned about our AWOL artist, I went through the facts of the case like a lawyer. I used my computer logs to show I'd picked up the artist at 9:03 a.m., called somebody about his next appointment and informed people about where he had to be. I was able not just to tell, but to show that I had my bases covered as best I could, and that the other team members needed to step up.

It was easy to see if people in promotions were performing at their jobs. Every day, the BDS report would tell the number of spins our records got on radio. If the work wasn't getting done, the count was low. People weren't hearing our songs on the radio and records weren't getting sold.

But I wanted Russell and Lyor to understand exactly what went down to get those spins. Every week, I typed a six-page memo detailing every significant event that related to how well my artists did. If an artist went on a radio interview I'd write down what time, for how long, what he said, and who called in. If there was a college summer jam, I'd say what the street teams did to promote it, from the colors of the posters at the bus stop to the type of plane we hired to write the artist's name in the sky.

The memos were a necessary way of keeping track of how budgets were spent and how effective our efforts were. In those early days, we were a small company. We couldn't afford to throw money around on ineffective ideas. Everyone in management was supposed to write one except for me. I was too junior. But I did the reports anyway. While others saw it as a chore, I saw it was my golden opportunity to create a record of my achievements.

Thomas Lytle and Mike Kyser, who were above me in promotions, saw what I was doing and decided to sit back on the smaller job. Rumor has it, they figured, "Great, Kevin's doing it now; we'll put our names on his report," but I'll never know for sure.

As the story goes, Russell called them out. He said, "What kind of a fool do you think I am? You guys never handed in a typed report before. This is the work of that new kid, Kevin Liles!"

My work spoke for me. My addiction to detail got me noticed. Within a year I was managing promotions on both the East Coast and the West Coast. Thomas got so sick with pneumonia he had to be hospitalized. He figured the pace was killing him so he stepped back and tapped me as the next national promotions director. I was moving in the right direction.

Don't Bite the Distraction

Focus, focus, focus. It may seem obvious, but every day I am amazed at how otherwise intelligent people fail to realize how important it is to pay attention to what they are doing.

It's so easy to get distracted, especially in these times of two-ways, Sidekicks, text messaging, cell phones. I admit I struggle with it. People bitch at me all the time because my eyes are drawn to the ten urgent messages coming through on my Blackberry while I'm in the middle of a conversation with a live person. It's just plain wrong not to focus on that person who is in the room with you, whether you're having a meeting in your office or you're out somewhere having dinner.

But the epidemic of inattention is getting out of control. Every week at Def Jam we used to have what we called the 911, and what later came to be known as the "Focus Meeting." All the department heads and key players would get together in Lyor's office or a conference room to discuss all the things that had to be done that week and brainstorm on some problems that needed to be solved.

These meetings were critical. Our business is so crazy, with so many fires burning simultaneously and so many artists with different personalities and issues to be dealt with, that it's the only time we're all able to get together in a room and talk it through as a team. It was our one chance to huddle and hear the coach call the play.

Before any of these meetings would start, I'd do what I almost never do: I'd switch off my Blackberry. But no matter what common sense and common courtesy would dictate, members of the management team did not follow my lead. Not only would their phones ring, they'd ANSWER those calls in the middle of our huddle! I actually had to point out to them that if they did nothing else in a Focus Meeting they were expected to at least FOCUS!

Muddy thinking comes across as a total lack of professionalism. So fix it. If you need to tell your boss something, think about it beforehand so that you can boil down every important point into key phrases. Don't get distracted and blabber on. Busy lips don't get heard.

Your boss will be more impressed that you troubled yourself to think about the message before taking up his time. If you have to make ten follow-up calls to clients, don't be vibing with friends over the Internet. Switch off the computer and get on the phone. Everyone makes mistakes, but those who are focused limit the ones they make and figure out how to get things straight.

Focus is tough to maintain because it happens on two levels. There's the kind of focus you need to come correct with the task put in front of you, and there's the sense of mission and urgency that you need to sustain as you handle the day-to-day and keep a focused eye on the prize.

Some people are naturally more focused than others. But if you have a short attention span or a low boredom threshold, you can discipline your mind. Tell yourself when you start the day what it is you want to accomplish. Remind yourself on a regular basis, and don't go home until it's done.

Every morning Reverend Run, aka Joey Simmons of Run DMC, one of the biggest rappers in the history of hip hop, sends me a daily dose on my Blackberry. One of the best ones lately was a reminder to me that despite all the changes going on at Def Jam, the new CEO, L.A. Reid, the downsizing that had to be done and the merging of corporate cultures, I shouldn't lose sight of my own personal mission.

"Keep your eye on the prize," he said. "Don't give in to temptation. You have the power to complete the mission if you believe you can. You have the power to push away all the lesser things that compete for your attention. While everyone around him was caught up in the daily diversions and pleasures of life, where was Thomas Edison? He was in his workshop, running 10,000 experiments to perfect the light bulb and changing the course of history. Make a difference. Stay on it. Don't taste the fruit. Don't bite the distraction!"

Probably one of the best examples of someone in the hip-hop culture who is focused is Beyoncé Knowles. She is the hottest female singer and dancer with a burgeoning career in movies. Through disciplined thought and disciplined action, she's realizing her goal of becoming a triple threat.

Beyoncé was taught how to be single-minded from the time she first picked up a mic. She was lucky to have a father like

Matthew Knowles, who made the commitment to his daughter and his niece, Kelly Rowland, from the moment he learned what their true passion was.

He gave up a six-figure salary at Xerox so he could help them achieve their goals. The family scaled down from a big suburban house and fancy car so that Beyoncé, her friend and her cousin could have their dream. Her parents asked for only one thing in return—focus.

When Beyoncé was just nine years old, Matthew made her practice three to four hours a day. He made the girls in the group sing and jog at the same time, so that when they went on the stage they could do what so few performers can do these days—maintain the momentum throughout. Most pop singers lip-sync when they do fast dance numbers. Not Destiny's Child. Not Beyoncé.

While he insists he's not a stage parent and would have found a way to buy a hospital if Beyoncé expressed a passion to be a doctor, Matthew does admit he's tough. But it's discipline with a purpose. He wanted to instill in those girls the drive to succeed at their dreams.

Beyoncé's biggest lesson on the temptation of distraction came when she was thirteen. Matthew had set up a performance for someone in charge of discovering and developing talent for Columbia Records. This music executive was coming into Houston just for the day. But it was hot the night before, so the girls decided they were going to go swimming.

Matthew warned them that they were making a choice that could affect how the next day would go. But he allowed them to go. Sure enough, the next morning the girls sucked. It was one of the most critical performances of their young careers, and they were croaking, literally.

"I stopped them right there in the middle of the performance," Matthew told me. "'This is an example of consequence,' I said. Then I made them go to the bathroom to blow their noses and get the phlegm off their vocal chords.

"Beyoncé was in the worst shape because she gets sinus infections, and the swimming brought it on again. I made them get focused by singing a cappella. Then they nailed it. We showed the tape to the folks at Columbia's head office and they wanted to sign."

Playing your position and maintaining that level of commitment and focus is one of the hardest things you'll ever do. Most people lack the attention span to keep it up nonstop. But it's so necessary. From the most complex deal to a conversation with your boss, you've got to pay close attention to what's in front of you.

When I was putting together Def Jam's record deal with Jamal "Shyne" Barrows, a call came through on my Blackberry while I was driving to New Jersey for a football game. It was Shyne calling from his prison cell in upstate New York, anxious to know the terms of his record deal and how his incarceration would affect the business we were about to enter into with him.

It was a delicate situation. Any wrong word could have set him off and put him into the hands of one of the dozens of other record labels trying to sign him. I had two of my assistants and a lawyer listening on separate lines while I conducted a negotiation that could have turned on a dime at any second.

I was using two phones at once. I had to be focused on the details of the deal, put Shyne at ease and check in with my team, all the while making sure to press the mute button at the right times.

People riding in the car with me said they were exhausted just listening to that transaction. But I was so in the zone and focused on the mission that it just flowed. I made the most talked-about record deal of the year.

Irv "Gotti" Lorenzo calls it "staying ignorant." He means that when there is a mission you've got to maintain a willful blindness to all the less important or urgent stuff that is going on around you. He's CEO of his own multimillion-dollar record label now. But when he has to break and produce a new artist, he withdraws from everyone and everything until he's finished the creative process.

"I just switch off to other people," Irv told me. "I don't want anyone to talk to me. F___ all that stuff outside the studio. When I'm in that place I don't care about anyone or anything else."

The most successful people in life find a way to keep focused. They keep reminding themselves of their ultimate goal.

I want to be the CEO of hip hop. I want to have a hand in building a media giant that goes way beyond the record industry. I want to create the Disney of tomorrow. I want to build a $100 million trust so that my children and my children's children can give away money to the communities that need a helping hand. I want to set the example for taking responsibility and holding myself accountable. Therefore I will not bite the distraction.

Stop Flossin'

The higher up you go, the easier it is to lose focus and edge. If you let yourself get puffed up you cut off the oxygen to your brain. It stops you from thinking straight.

I may be at the top of my game now, but if I ever lose my sense of humility, I'll slip and fall. One of the first rules of hip hop is that you never forget where you came from. As soon as a rap artist gets to thinking he's too big, he loses his fan base. The same rule applies in any business.

Sam Walton, the founder of Wal-Mart, the biggest retailer in the world, called it "thinking small."

"The bigger Wal-Mart gets, the more essential it is that we think small," he writes in his book, *Made in America*.

> Because that's exactly how we have become a huge corporation—by not acting like one. Above all, we are small-town merchants, and I can't tell you how important it is for us to remember—when we puff up our chests and brag about all those huge sales and profits—that they were all made one day at a time, one store at a time, mostly by the hard work, good attitude and teamwork of all those hourly associates and their store managers, as well as by all those folks in the distribution centers. If we ever get carried away with how important we are because we're a great big $50 billion chain—instead of one store in Blytheville, Arkansas or McComb, Mississippi or Oak Ridge, Tennessee—then you probably can close the book on us.

Once you start thinking you're too important, the small but necessary tasks don't get done. Before you know it, you're not handling your business. Someone else is.

When Lyor and Russell decided to offer me the title of president, I didn't even want it. I didn't want the other people on the team I'd come up with to feel awkward about reporting to me. I didn't want them to think that I'd gotten too big.

Despite my title, I never asked the people who worked for me to do anything that I wasn't willing to do myself. If I have to step somewhere I don't let pride block my path. People laugh at me because if I see a piece of paper on the floor, I pick it up. I can't help myself! If I see it needs to be done, I do it. You wouldn't leave trash on the floor of your own home, would you? Why should the office be any different?

I might be the boss, but I've mopped the stage before one of our artists has stepped on to perform. The floor was slick and I didn't see anyone else out wiping it down, so I went to it. Was I going to let my sense of self-importance contribute to someone I was responsible for slipping and hurting himself? Hell no!

I would do, and have done, just about anything because I believed in the mission of the label I worked for. I would do, and have done, everything I could to get the job done right.

When I delivered newspapers as a kid, I thought about whether my neighbor wanted it delivered on the doorstep, inside the screen door or through the letter box. Seeing other boys and girls toss the *Baltimore Sun* onto the bottom of somebody's driveway upset me. What if it rained? I couldn't understand how they could not care.

"But Kevin, don't sweat it, it's just a newspaper," Joey, one of the delivery boys, said. "If it misses the porch, who gives a damn?"

I did. Maybe it was just a paper route, but it was *my* paper route. Therefore, I cared.

If I didn't care, I'd hear about it from my mother. I've caught hell for not completing my chores properly. Once, when I was sixteen, I didn't bother to load the dishwasher. I figured I had better things to do. I was hanging out in the basement writing some rap lyrics. I was tired of doing what my family needed of me, so I rebelled and did what I wanted to do.

When my mother got home, she was mad. I had to leave the house that night! I called my buddies to come and pick me up so I could sleep at my grandmother's house. My family team needed me to play my position, but I didn't so I suffered the consequences. Loading the dishwasher may not have been a big deal, but, to my mom, failure to keep a promise was a serious matter. To her, my negligence was a sign of arrogance and disrespect.

It doesn't matter if you're scrubbing toilets in a restaurant or picking up trash from the streets. Whatever you do in life deserves your best effort, because YOU are doing it. You express what kind of person you are by doing an honest day's work. If you don't take pride in what you do, you don't have pride in yourself.

Grinding at the small stuff doesn't always bring in the Benjamins. But if you keep at it long enough and keep the faith, it will. Meanwhile, it builds the character you need to handle success when it finally comes.

Work Is the Fun Part

If something can be done better, make the improvement. Do it all over again if need be. Be Martha Stewart. Strive for perfection in every little thing you do. (Just don't lie to the feds about it!) The reward is in the work itself, not the results.

Russell still can't remember anything about the day he sold Def Jam to Universal in 1998. That day when his net worth exploded to more than $500 million is just a blur. It was the years spent building up the label to the point where fourteen artists were earning more in revenue than the established company looking to take it over. That stuck in Russell's memory. It was the long hours of negotiations with potential buyers. It was the weekends on his cell phone in the days, weeks and months leading up to the sale, trying to get the best deal for his company, his family and himself.

In 2004 Russell went on to make a pile of cash—$140 million—from selling his clothing line, Phat Farm, but he doesn't remember feeling especially good about it. In fact, it was a kind of downer.

"If anything, we were a little depressed," he said. "When the big check or the payoff comes, then you have to find some other goals. We build the thing and sell the thing, then its over and all that sh__ we thought we wanted don't mean sh__. What people call the finest hour, the biggest success, removes some big focus, and focuses are fun."

The fun is in all those little details, those small jobs that make up the goal.

Whenever he meets a kid looking for advice about following in his path and getting into the music business, this is what he tells them:

"Put your head down, work and check your ego at the door. If the floor's dirty, get up off your ass and sweep it now. Don't wait for someone to give you that golden opportunity. That's bull. There's always a job waiting to be done, so do it!"

Those kids look so surprised to hear him say that. They see Russell, the godfather of hip hop, with his gorgeous model wife, his parties in the Caribbean, looking fly in all the magazines and they can't compute. They think it was easy. But behind every great success there is a lifetime of doing the job right through hard work.

Later on in life, you're going to appreciate all that you have because you know how hard you had to work for it. You'll learn to respect and recognize that same work ethic in others. You'll gain an instinct for the small details that can make or break an organization. You'll look back on the come-up and realize that, in fact, you actually enjoyed all those hours you put in.

When you've earned that perspective, you'll be ready to lead.

RULE 5

What: Play Your Position

Why: Don't act like you're too good for it. Have the humility and respect to do your job to the best of your ability, whether it's digging ditches or answering the phone. That's how all great leaders get started.

How: Think about the higher cause and play for the team. Serve, focus and pay attention to detail. Find ways to make the boss look good. Search for what needs to be done. When the whole organization does well, it will lift you up.

But: Once you reach the higher position, don't forget where you came from. Stay grounded to keep your focus and edge.

Embrace the Struggle

It's the hard knock life for us

Stead of treated . . . we get tricked

Stead of kisses . . . we get kicked.

—Jay-Z, "Hard Knock Life"

Don't stress the hard knocks in your life. You've got to love the hard times. There is good and bad in everything, but if we can learn from our struggles and mistakes, we aren't just surviving, we're on our way to thriving.

Anyone who has ever achieved true success can tell you it was the string of failures and misfortunes before the breakthrough that made them who they are. Whether it's your own mistake, someone got one over on you or the hardship just happened, you have three choices: play the victim and whine about it, blame the bastard and kick him in the head or embrace it for what it truly is: a blessing.

Hardship gives us the gift of perspective. When you hit an

obstacle and somehow manage to feel your way around it, you cover more ground and see new ways of doing things that you might miss if success comes too easily. "Tryin' to make it through" is a positive process. We stumble so that when we get back up again we can walk taller and stronger. We fall down, but we get up.

No matter how bad it gets, there is always a flip side. Setbacks can actually push you forward into a whole different orbit.

Def Jam is a case in point. It wouldn't exist if it weren't for the struggle. Russell wanted to be a music executive, but no one from the big record labels wanted to hire a scruffy kid raw from the streets, no matter how talented a producer, promoter and visionary he was. That dissing prompted him to start his own label, a different kind of record company that could be true to our culture.

Ludacris was a deejay in Atlanta who knew he had talent as a rap artist. But he couldn't get anyone to sign him. He went from record label to record label. They all said no. But that rejection fueled his faith in himself. He put up his own money to produce his first album. It was a hit. Suddenly, everyone wanted to sign him. Because he'd been forced to set up on his own, he knew the business better and was in a position to ask for a better cut when he finally signed with us.

Our most successful artists are here today because of the struggle. As much as some people like to hate some of our hardcore rap lyrics, they reflect the truth about life in the streets. The kids who buy music relate to it because it's real. The artists express a reality—the war on poverty, the horror of kids being raised in crack houses, parents getting arrested, kids joining drug gangs—that needs to be faced and addressed. Through it all, this struggle produces art.

Instead of killing people, hustling or stealing, rappers mine their hardships for artistic material. They stay alive through the poetry they write alone in their rooms, away from the trouble. Suffering makes their storytelling a sound track to their everyday reality.

Early on in his success, Jay always found it necessary to speak about his pain. His struggle was his everyday reality. He was always going through something. He'd been facing the disappointment of failed friendships that can sometimes be part of the baggage of success. He told the truth that hard times come no matter how far we've made it.

Like so many artists who've come up from poverty, he was struggling to adjust to the fact that, when you've made it, people are going to use you, friends are going to betray you, and lovers aren't going to love you for who you are. All that money and fame doesn't quite bring you the happiness you thought it would. The result is his *Blueprint* album, which has some of the most memorable joints in hip-hop music:

> **I can't see 'em comin down my eyes**
> **So I gotta make the song cry . . .**

Jay is just one of many great rap artists who has found a way to spin his pain into the profound.

Misfortune Can Motivate

The people I respect most in the world came up and succeeded in life despite and even because of the sadness and hardship they faced back in the day.

As I mentioned, Roy Williams, a safety for the Dallas Cowboys, seems to have it all now: the money and glory of being in the NFL. Sportswriters call this guy a "freak" because he is so physically perfect. He's a star on and off the field.

But when I first met him in 2001, when he was just twenty, I recognized an old soul. Like so many successful black athletes, he survived the same struggle that so many hip-hop artists went through. Roy's family was solid, like mine, but he came up surrounded by negative influences.

He escaped a life in the streets through talent and sheer force of will. His mom had to work, so as a young boy he stayed at his aunt's house during the day. His aunt was a crack addict and a dealer.

"Every hour on the hour, strange men would come to the door and ask me, 'Where's your auntie at?'" Roy told me over dinner one evening. "Any time the house could have been shot up. I remember going into the dining room and seeing a big pile of white powder. I thought it was baby powder so I rubbed it on my arms. It was crack cocaine."

Roy's cousins became addicts. He used to watch them drink and smoke crack in the street outside. That didn't impress him. He thought they looked stupid. Watching them ruin their lives, and seeing the plight of so many homeless families where he grew up, made him determined to be on television and make lots of money so that he could give his mother, father and sister a comfortable life and protect them from poverty.

Roy got himself a scholarship to the University of Oklahoma, practiced and trained seven hours a day just in the off-season, kept up his grades, blew all the statistics off the charts and became the best football safety the school had ever seen.

But he doesn't take his success in the NFL for granted. It's a means to an even greater end. He's working on his life after football. He's not blowing his paycheck on a Bentley. He's investing his money and planning a future so that he can retire his mother and give back to the community. Witnessing how poverty can destroy the lives of children, he's become a spokesman for the Boys and Girls Clubs of America and the United

Way. He has also started his own foundation, Safety Net, to help single mothers like his sister.

Struggle has taught him compassion. Even though money was always tight in his own family, they gave what they could. Roy's mother took him to homeless shelters to serve meals to families much less fortunate than theirs.

"Watching their faces, and how joyful they were to get a hot dinner, made me all the more determined to better myself so that I could take care of myself, my family and those less fortunate," Roy said.

People say nice words like that every day. But when you live through it, it really means something. The experience made him the winner he is today.

Setbacks . . . Set You Up

Sometimes you've got to have lows to be able to understand the highs. You need to learn what success is, and know the difference between failure and progress.

I was sixteen when my rap group Numarx put out its first record out on KMA. We used to call it "Kiss My Ass Records." The single, called "Bus It," didn't go all the way like we desperately hoped it would. We sold maybe a few hundred copies, and barely recouped the money we'd invested in ourselves.

My homeboy, Rod, was so disappointed he was ready to walk away. I said, "Look, we *are* talented, it's just not our time yet."

Sometimes you don't get your desired result at first. But without realizing it you are taking steps toward your goal. You have to know when and what progress is. Sometimes, progress can be the needle moving a little bit to the right. Sometimes, instead of a six-digit increase, it's a five-digit increase.

Just because they don't achieve that desired result or attain perceived success right away, some people give up. But the difference between success and failure can be little more than a minute. The next time you try, it could all come together. Giving up too soon is the real failure.

In fact, the record got us noticed and taught us a lot about how you put an album together. Later on we signed with a better production company, started producing our own albums and eventually had a few hits.

At Def Jam, we took two steps forward, three steps backward, five steps sideways and ten leaps straight up. We experimented with all kinds of dumb-ass concepts like Russell's "horrorcore" rap, a kind of cheesy gothic hip hop that went nowhere. Then there was the $2 million mistake when we made Sisqo's "Unleash the Dragon" video.

Sisqo had the big idea to make a ten-minute video action feature like Michael Jackson's "Thriller," complete with Sisqo running up a building to fight a giant fire-breathing mechanical dragon. It looked like *Puff the Magic Dragon* meets *Godzilla*. We had to shelve it.

As happens with so many other projects, we had to write it off. As Lyor said after a similar video disaster, "If it ain't right, it ain't right, and it ain't going out of the effing building."

You have to take risks in a creative business. We've messed up spectacularly as we've tested out what does and doesn't work. But each time we've gotten wiser. That's how you grow.

The School of Hard Knocks

Suffering is just another form of education. Failing a few times makes you less afraid of making mistakes. You take more risks. You stand up. That's healthy. Being human and acknowledging the error of your ways also teaches you humility in the face of success.

Back in the day, when Numarx was performing all over Baltimore and people were tripping over themselves to be with our crew, I had the opportunity to host a local hip-hop show on television. I figured that just by showing up I'd get the job. Everyone knew me. I was already a local hip-hop star.

"F___ it," I said to myself. "I'm Kevin Liles."

I didn't prepare. I didn't research. I didn't schmooze. I was horrible, so of course they turned me down.

That failure taught me not to take any situation for granted. No matter who you are, you'd better plan and do your homework. By the time an opportunity came around to get on Def Jam's payroll, I knew better. That's why I had all the sh__. Like I said before, I showed up with those briefcases full of pie charts and graphs. I *over*prepared!

My own rise through the ranks of Def Jam was fast, but I made my fair share of mistakes along the way. Just a year into my position as head of promotions in Baltimore, I had what I thought was the brilliant idea that we needed to do a hip-hop concert tour. I decided we'd take Redman, Method Man and Onyx across the U.S.

I wanted kids to see these artists live. A backlash against rap artists in the early '90s made it hard to fill arenas. There was this perception, not exactly fair, that our music incited more violence than your average rock concert. Parents were keeping their kids at home. People who wanted to see their artist had to watch BET or MTV. I was determined to change that.

I told Lyor the whole thing would cost about $30,000. What I didn't consider was how hard it was going to be to get all of these artists to wake up, catch the bus and be where they were supposed to be on time. We were running so late I had to fly them to different cities at thousands of dollars a plane ticket. Instead of making money, the whole project ended up costing Def Jam about $300,000!

That was a ton of money for us back then. My bad planning

hurt Def Jam a lot. My ass could have been fired. At the end of the tour, when I'd tallied up the costs and realized what a disastrous mistake I'd made, I dreaded the moment I would have to own up and face Lyor.

Now Lyor has a reputation for being fierce. He's intimidating as hell with his six-foot three-inch frame. Behind his desk hangs a spooky portrait of Dracula that looks just like him. If he truly thinks you've done wrong, he'll light up his cigar, stare right through you and cut you a new asshole with a few sharp words.

But when I told him what happened, he said, "Kevin, I made some of the same mistakes."

He appreciated how hard I was grinding. He also understood that no one was being harder on me than me for making an honest mistake. Lyor's reaction to my error taught me how to be a better manager and a better person. Experiencing failure and the acceptance of what followed taught me to show the same compassion and perspective when somebody under me screwed up.

It's one thing to do your best and fall short of your goal. It's quite another to put in a BS effort and expect to succeed. I can see whether someone is sincerely trying, or just being slick with it. Most bosses can tell when you've done your utmost, whatever the end result.

I also learned one of the best things I could have possibly learned early in my career: always, *always* plan for the worst. No matter how well you cross your *t*'s and dot your *i*'s, it's going to cost more. Guaranteed. Now, when I calculate a concert or a video shoot is going to cost $100,000, I take into consideration certain intangibles and budget for $150,000.

The rest of my Def Jam family rode me about it for months afterward. When I first started in the New York office they viewed me as some Goody Two-shoes who was brought in to show them all up by example. Well, as a matter of fact I was. But one huge lapse became their opportunity to remind me of the fact that I wasn't so perfect.

I won't lie to you. That killed me. To this day, I hate being wrong and I hate losing. But the experience humbled me. It prepared me for success.

Own It

It's okay to admit when you're wrong. An enlightened manager understands that owning the failure and growing from it is a sign of integrity and strength.

Doug Morris, CEO of Universal Music Group and one of the biggest bosses in the industry, told me that he always looks at the intent behind the error. If it's malicious, no matter how small the problem or how slight the slight, he's much less willing to overlook it than if someone makes a big mess out of wrongheaded good intentions.

That doesn't mean you should repeat a string of mistakes. A few errors are okay if you take responsibility and fix them. But do it again, and again, and again, and eventually I'd have to fire you. It means you either do not care, you are not paying attention, you are not listening, you are not learning from your mistakes or you are just straight-up incompetent. As a boss, I hate not being heard by my employees. Carelessness makes me crazy.

I'm not saying that you should run to your boss every time some little thing goes wrong. If you can fix it, *fix* it. Next issue!

Disclose the smaller errors and how you resolved them after the fact. You will have shown that you're honest but also resourceful enough to catch the error and make repairs. I'd still want you to discuss the mistakes with me, even the small five-dollar ones, but I'm not going to dwell on them. Instead, I'll appreciate the fact that you handled your business and continue to learn from the mishaps and mistakes.

But if it's something big, you've got to show and tell. If my head of publicity can't get Ashanti on the cover of *Vibe* magazine in time for the release of her new album, she'd better get me involved. If there's a $5 million dollar mistake and I find out about it afterward, the person who tried to cover up is going to get on my bad side.

Meant to Be

I did countless things when I was growing up that were not wise. Some people might say some of my stunts were downright foolish. I look back at my hustling days now and say, "What the hell was I thinking?" But somehow I learned what I was supposed to learn from those moments of youthful stupidity.

When I was twelve I got locked up in the back of a store for stealing. The owner caught me and kept me in there for a while to think about what I'd done. I can't even remember exactly what it was I was trying to steal. It was something small like a candy bar. But I didn't need to steal it. I had the money. I just had an itch to scratch.

Thank God he decided not to call the cops and have me arrested. He just made me pay for the item and sent me on my way. He must have taken pity on me. Realizing the consequences of my pointless, reckless actions scared me straight. For a while.

From my mid-teens until the time I was about nineteen, I dabbled in the game. We moved the usual list of products: dope, car radios, rims, guns, whatever could bring in a few thousand dollars at a time.

We had a little crew running around the streets of West Baltimore—me, Tuffy, Rod and some other guys. It wasn't a gang. We weren't into violence. We were just hustlers. It was all for the thrill. We had a network of associates sprinkled all over town involved in various types of capers, some more serious than others. Different crews were moving different products.

We were wrong but, when we were growing up, it was the norm. My friends and I came from stable homes and weren't exactly poor, but, nevertheless, hustling was the life we were exposed to on the streets where we came up. We took the path of least resistance.

Back then the guy we saw on the corner in the fly sweatsuit and the Benz wasn't some music executive or pro athlete, he was a drug dealer. That's the guy we aspired to be like. He had the money, the cars and the girls.

I wanted to try a few things. The excitement and the opportunity to make a fast buck were what lured me to the game. I didn't need the money. I didn't hustle to pay the bills. I always had legitimate jobs. At the same time, back then, I didn't see many other ways to make a few thousand in a lump sum.

One night we decided we needed a car radio so we broke into a parked car in a lot on the outskirts of town. I was in the driver's seat, unscrewing the stereo. My friend and fellow Numarx member, Darryl Mimms, aka Junie Jam, was in the passenger seat. Whenever a car drove by, we'd duck our heads down. All of a sudden, I saw red lights. I thought to myself, "Oh sh__! It's a siren! This is it. The cops are here and we're all going to get arrested!"

Jam screamed, "Damn! Kevin, Kevin, get your foot off the brake!"

I didn't respect the hustle enough to get deep into it. I only wanted to be a part of the lives of my homeboys. I wanted to vibe with the other kids in the streets. I didn't want to let myself be taken over by the street. I wanted to be involved just enough to build my little network of "associates," then go home.

One time there was a serious beef between crews from our

corner, at Liberty Heights, and rival gangs from another neighborhood in Baltimore. All the little crews assembled at a neutral spot—some restaurant—to discuss our differences. It didn't go well. At any given moment I was terrified somebody was going to draw a knife or open fire.

Weeks later I was at a club dancing with some random young lady. A guy came along and interrupted us, letting me know she was his girl. I said that was cool, I didn't know she was his girl, and walked away. A few minutes later he came over to my friends and me on the other side of the dance floor.

"My girl said you don't like what I have on," he said.

"What the f___ are you talkin' about?" I replied. I really had no idea what he was talking about.

"My girl said you don't like what I have on," he repeated, with his woman standing behind him rolling her eyes as if to say, "He's an asshole."

"Look man, I'm sorry I danced with your girl," I said. "But you should be on point and don't leave her alone."

Next thing I knew, all hell broke loose. Everybody and their crews were fighting each other.

None of it made sense to me at the time. Then I found out that this guy was from the same gang our associate crews were beefing with a few weeks earlier. He'd seen me on the day when all the other guys from Liberty Heights and Gwynn Oaks broke out into a beef and just assumed I was his enemy.

It taught me that when you're hustling you'd better be careful about where you go and who you associate with, because no matter how hard you try to stay out of the violence, being in the game is going to come back to bite you. You could be in deep even if you think you're staying on the sidelines.

Looking back now, I believe my experience in the game is why, to this day, I can go into any situation and feel like I can work it out. I've already faced life-and-death situations.

In many ways, I admired those friends who were good at the hustle. They knew how to think fast on their feet. They knew how to negotiate a deal that's make or break. We shouldn't judge them. We don't know what bills they had to pay, or who they had to support. We don't know their sorrows.

But I don't recommend street hustling. In that game, you're lucky to survive past the age of twenty-three. Serious hustlers either get hooked on their own dope, lose decades out of their lives in prison or come to a violent end. So many of the guys I knew back then are dead.

I've been shot at. I've stood too close to guys who owed money and been caught in the crossfire. I've seen friends gunned down. So has Rod. He was at a basketball game in a rival neighborhood when one of our close buddies got into an argument with someone from the opposing team. The coach sent the guy our friend was arguing with off the court. Half an hour later, this guy came back and shot our friend, execution-style, in the head.

At the funeral, Rod said he wondered why his life was spared and not our friend's. I'd wondered myself why I hadn't been there that day. I might have tried to stop the fight and gotten myself killed.

"Rod, we were meant to survive this," I said. "This means we have to do something with our lives."

Don't Be Afraid of the Dark

It's not always easy to see the good in hard times. But if you look deep enough, you'll find it.

When I was going through it last year after my departure from Def Jam, Reverend Run sent me this daily dose message that said:

Don't be afraid of the dark! Before anything worthwhile is

acquired, you must experience a dark period. Right before a breakthrough there is usually a great pain. Ask any woman who gave birth to a child. Darkness is not a bad thing. The dark room is necessary for any good picture to get developed. The Bible says, "Weeping lasts for a night but joy cometh in the morning!"

Jamal "Shyne" Barrow's dark room was a prison cell up in Dannemorea, New York. His great pain started one night in December 1999 when he was kicking it in a Manhattan night-club with P. Diddy and Jennifer Lopez. It was just after Christ-mas and everyone was in a party mood until a scuffle started. All hell broke loose and Shyne fired his burner. A lot of people suffered that night.

Shyne said he feared for his life and was just protecting him-self. The facts of the prosecution's case against Shyne were questionable. It's possible that as many as three people fired their guns, but Shyne was the only one who ended up getting charged and doing hard time for reckless endangerment, reck-less assault and weapons possession.

A lot of young rappers have gotten into the habit of carrying a piece. They've lived with threats their whole lives. Successful artists have been slain at their peak. Homeboys from the 'hood get jealous. Old enemies want to bring you down. The war of poverty can make people ruthless.

Shyne was almost a casualty of this war. He grew up in juve-nile homes, witnessing crack deals go down when he was just nine. When he was thirteen he saw his friend get shot dead right in front of him. He got shot up when he was just fifteen. Bullets ripped his shoulder to shreds and he nearly bled to death. So when it went down that winter night, his old survival instincts kicked in.

"I went back to square one," he said in an interview with *XXL* magazine while the trial was going on. "I went back to when I was on the block and the n____ I had a beef with lived right next door. And when I had to walk outside every day, how it had to go down . . . I'm thinkin' about when I was lying there in the f_____ pool of blood, my shoulder ripped off, taking myself to the hospital. I'm like, 'Yo, how we got back here?' "

Who knows what really happened that night in the club. I wasn't there. I didn't live through Shyne's struggle. If my back was against the wall, I don't know what I would do. I don't judge my homeboy, I pray for him. But I'm more interested in the stand-up way he has conducted himself ever since that fateful night.

Shyne could have saved his own ass by testifying against other people, but he refused. He wasn't taking anyone down with him. He accepted responsibility for having and firing a weapon that night. He took his punishment.

Waiting for the trial, he channeled his frustration and grief into writing rhymes. They express anger, rage, his sense of injustice, his feelings of regret for his own hand in those unfortunate events. A true artist, Shyne turned what could have become destructive into something creative.

While we were negotiating his record deal in the spring of 2004, he called me from prison. He wanted me to understand how much he was feeling the importance of what we were doing. "Yo, Kevin, this is all I got," he said. "My music, that's my freedom. My art is my way to communicate to the outside world because I'm not there."

Every chance he gets, through print and radio interviews, he tries to reach out to young fans and tell them not to make his mistakes, not to carry a burner, to stay out of trouble. He's devastated by the grief his situation brought on his mother. He takes responsibility for that and he has plenty he wants to say about it in his last album, *Godfather Buried Alive*.

He's making big plans for his new life on the outside. He's formed his own label, Gangland Records, to give other people chances and nurture talent. He's always had a business sense, but now he has the opportunity to express it. He's planning and thinking through every detail of his artistic comeback to make sure he does it right this time around.

He's made some right decisions and some wrong decisions, but he acknowledges that in life you make both types of choices and live and learn from their consequences. That's why he's surrounding himself with people he trusts and making sure he stays in situations that are clean and safe. He's got religion. He wants his life back for good this time, and I believe he's going to get it, even if he has to finish out the six years left in his sentence.

That's the kind of breakthrough that comes from hard times.

The Truth in Tragedy

Even the worst moments in life, like the death of an icon, tell us something that we need to know to be able to move forward, although it might not be obvious at the time.

The day Tupac Shakur died, I felt a pain go through me. It was September 1996. I was in the middle of my grind years at Def Jam. I was constantly on the road promoting our artists. I was back and forth between the East Coast and L.A., trying to build the label's West Coast office. There was an East Coast–West Coast rivalry among rap labels—Bad Boy and Death Row—and it was turning ugly.

I sat on the edge of the bed in some anonymous hotel, I forget where, and flicked on CNN. Someone driving by in a Cadillac shot Tupac in the chest. Right there on the Vegas strip, smack in front of hundreds of people, a great artist was struck down in a cold-blooded execution.

Tupac was one of those rappers who'd lived the violence and struggle of the gangsta life. He grew up dirt poor and his come-up was a hard one. He'd sold $60 million worth of albums by the time of his death, but he never escaped the life of struggle.

Tupac was the real thing. He was the original artist raw from the streets. He wasn't just doing the art of rap. He was art itself. He lived life on the edge. His words painted pictures of the brutality of ghetto life in rhymes like "Brenda's Got a Baby" and "Trapped," in 1991. In 1995, before he went away for sexual assault, he faced his fear in music with the joint, "Me Against the World."

His own life was the biggest case study. He would have bewildered any scientist or psychiatrist. Whatever he was thinking was where we all needed to be, but tragically not where he was. I got chills when I first heard "Blasphemy," which became a hit after his death. His rhyme was eerily prophetic:

> Dear Lord, don't let me die tonight . . .
> Do what you gotta do, but know you gotta find a way to change:
> Get out of the game . . .

Tupac deserves a Purple Heart. He was a soldier. He should have been honored. In this war on poverty his was one of the lives sacrificed to bring awareness and teach us how to be better. But back then people weren't ready to change. In my heart I knew it was going to get worse. It did.

Some people say it was the day President Kennedy died. Other people's lives were changed the day Martin Luther King died. I'll always remember exactly where I was the day that the Notorious B.I.G. died.

It was March 9, 1997. We'd just done this big, *big* party in

L.A. after the Soul Train awards. The night before, our artists did a show at the House of Blues. We were in the middle of the East Coast–West Coast rap rivalry thing.

We'd just seen Biggie a couple of hours before. *Vibe* magazine threw a party after the awards that got so crowded the police shut it down. Our Def Jam crew left early. We went back to Le Montrose Hotel, where we always stay. The next thing I knew, I got a page. "Biggie's been shot." Once again, it was a drive-by execution.

I was blown away. It was happening again. But my protective instincts kicked in. I'm in my hotel room thinking, "We've got to get everybody out of L.A." Everybody knew where we were staying. Biggie was friends with Foxy Brown, one of our artists. Everyone was staying there. I booked everyone out on the next flight to New York.

These deaths weren't necessary. They were senseless and sad. We'd lost enough in this game. But looking back, I think our culture changed for the better as a result of the tragedies.

Other rappers have died, but those two were so intrinsic to the culture. Jay-Z pays homage to Biggie and Tupac every time he does a concert. Their deaths created awareness. They quelled something that came damn close to a civil war in the world of hip hop. Biggie and Tupac mean so much to people and losing them was so devastating it made everything else seem trivial.

People finally started asking themselves, "Damn, what were we beefing about? East Coast, West Coast, what? Do we really need to die for that?" It was so dramatic that it made people wake up. I ran into one guy who asked me, "What difference does it make what coast I come from. I'm still poor and struggling to survive. Brothers are fighting over something they don't even own."

As a company, Def Jam also changed. We stayed away from

the beefing. We didn't want to get into who was bigger or who was better. We didn't want to outshine or be as flossy as some people are. We didn't want to beat people up. We wanted to do what our artists needed us to do, and that is work hard for them. From that moment, we became the blue-collar company. As Lyor stated, "We put on the overalls and became Amoco."

How could anything good come out of those slayings? You should have seen the headlines. Conservative, racist commentators were gloating that we were going to destroy ourselves and it would be the end of hip hop.

The *Chicago Tribune* was one of the worst culprits, with a headline after Tupac's death that said, IS GANGSTA RAP THROUGH? DEFECTIONS, DEATH AND LACK OF IDEAS MAY DO WHAT CENSORS COULDN'T.

It fed into all the bull that rap lyrics cause violence. To this day, despite widespread acceptance of hip hop in mainstream America and the simultaneous drop in murder rates across U.S. cities, the pundits still refuse to accept that our artists are merely expressing the painful truth of urban poverty and violence, not causing it.

Like Shyne says in his joint, "More or Less," "They don't do it cuz I rap about it / I rap about it cuz they do it."

Even though we've had a few well-publicized beefs since, we haven't destroyed each other. Our industry has flourished and expanded into all kinds of consumer and entertainment arenas, and our fallen soldiers are relatively few.

Of course, there are always going to be beefs among rap artists. Growing up poor, some of those guys hold on to that mentality of grasping for every dollar. It's still a screw-or-be-screwed world to them.

It doesn't do anything for anybody. But hip hop is a competitive thing. Rappers do battle in their lyrics, and sometimes it spills off of records. Some people can't see eye to eye. We have to be able to learn how to get money and allow each other to enjoy the same success.

Make it Make Sense

Seeing the light in the dark is never harder than when somebody close to you dies. As hard to accept as the deaths of Biggie and Tupac were, they weren't as personally painful to me as the slaying of Jam Master Jay. He was my close friend.

My relationship with Jay was threefold. I first came to his shows as a fan. When I was a rapper, I used to open for Run DMC in Baltimore. When I went from intern to full-time employee of Def Jam, Run DMC was my first charge. It was my job to take care of them, take them to radio interviews and schedule press conferences. They helped me get my start in the business.

Jay watched me grow up. We'd call each other on the holidays. When Joey Simmons, now Reverend Run, was going through it and deciding to become a man of the cloth, I gave him his first Bible. Jay always reminded me about that.

About three weeks before his death, in October 2002, Jay was hanging out with me in my office at Def Jam. Run DMC had long passed its peak and it was time to enter a new phase, so we were just talking about Jay's plans in life and the whole nine. There were no premonitions of doom. None of that. Jay, our pioneer in popularizing rap for the mainstream, was a peace-loving entrepreneur. He was all about survival and had love in the streets.

Then, for no reason the cops have been able to figure out, he was shot and killed in the streets of New York City. He was dead at thirty-seven. When a black man survives his first thirty years without getting shot, it's just not supposed to happen like that.

That day I was away on a tour with Lyor, who started his career in music as Run DMC's road manager. When we got the word we cut the tour short and came back to New York. It was a devastating time for all of us. All the kids from Hollis were like brothers to us. We thought, "Damn, is this ever going to end?"

But we had to realize that every day we're still living life, and every day someone is going to get murdered, whether it's a rapper or not. We may think we are bigger than life, but we're not. Whether you work on Wall Street or you are just some poor bastard getting mugged, you could suffer the same fate.

It bothers me that the police haven't solved any of these murders. The first two may have had some connection with the New York–L.A. rivalry, but I believe it's more complicated than that. These cases have been too easily dismissed, just because the victims were rap artists. Chris Rock jokes, "If you want to get away with murder, kill a rapper." I'd laugh if it wasn't so true.

Every day, if a young kid from the ghetto is in the wrong place at the wrong time, or "driving while black," the police are quick as lightning to investigate. Meanwhile the robber barons of some big mainstream businesses get away with bilking millions from ordinary investors and retirees.

Not a day goes by when I don't struggle with a sense of rage about how screwed up this is. It's life in America and it's time for a change. So my anger gives me energy. I don't dwell on what other people are doing to me; I make it happen so much that I can effect change.

I can't get caught up in that, "Oh woe is me, they are trying to bring the black man down; oh there are not enough jobs." I'm not having any of that. I'm going to create jobs and opportunity, and hopefully provide hope to the next generation.

RULE 6

What: Embrace the Struggle

Why: Learning to love the hard times can make you stronger, wiser and more willing to take risks.

How: A hard life can give you the motivation to better yourself. Mistakes can teach you how to do it better the next time. Tragedy can teach you tolerance. Hard knocks help you stand up.

But: Don't permit yourself to make careless mistakes. Admit when you've done wrong and be prepared to fix it.

Get
Connected

Deals come and go. Jobs are here today and gone tomorrow. But it's the relationships you build and the respect you earn from colleagues, friends and associates that stay with you. Get connected and build a personal network to last forever.

Business is fundamentally about transactions between people. If it's thriving, at the end of the day you get a check. But it takes at least two people to make a deal. Nine times out of ten, success is based on who you know and how well you are regarded by the people you come into contact with. Relationships are the foundation, bricks and mortar of most organizations. A firm handshake closes the deal.

Russell's friendship with one of the forefathers of rap, Kurtis Blow, and an extended network of other brothers from Hollis, helped launch him on the road to building Def Jam. Bob Johnson, the chairman and founder of Black Entertainment Television, started his media empire by building on relationships he had through his job as a lobbyist for the National Cable Television Association.

Bob's boss, the president of the NCTA, gave him $15,000 to help Bob launch his dream of television programs targeted at black audiences. Then Bob convinced the head of Tele-Communications Inc. to invest $500,000 in his project. Soon after, Bob met the president of UA–Columbia Cablevision at an annual convention. The guy was so impressed with Bob's plan, he said Bob could have the slots he owned on cable TV and satellite to use for the new channel. Getting connected was instrumental in making BET happen.

Networking is not to be confused with getting ahead through shameless ass-kissing. That's just politics. I'm not referring to the lucky-sperm club. Nepotism can help anyone get a foot in the door, no doubt, but it's not going to keep you inside the building. I'm talking about doing right by people, at all times. I'm talking about building a reputation for integrity.

That's why, when things went down between Jay-Z and R. Kelly during a concert tour last summer and R. Kelly walked off the stage at Madison Square Garden, the New York artists who were in the audience stepped up and performed alongside Jay.

Jay doesn't take crap from anyone, but over the years he's garnered a reputation for artistic and professional integrity. I was among Jay's friends who rushed backstage after the announcement was made to find out what he wanted to do. It took all of a few seconds for us to get those artists to perform. When I asked T.I., he said, "Yo, whatever Jay needs."

Mary J. Blige, Usher, Ja Rule and T.I. showed him the love and respect and made sure the show would go on. That's how it went down in city after city. Mary J. and P. Diddy did every date, Trick Daddy turned up in Miami, Jermaine Dupri got up on stage in Atlanta, and Snoop Dogg blessed us also.

Jay's unquestionable success and honesty gave him the opportunity to turn what was a disastrous moment for his fans into a great night of surprise entertainment, and hip-hop history was made.

Carry the Tray

In business, all things being even, promotions, contracts, commissions and mergers are based on trust and the belief that you will ultimately deliver. I'm talking about bestowing the gift of service that we all have to give in our day-to-day transactions.

Have you ever noticed that when you go for your morning coffee there is always one person who's seen you come in a few times and remembers you take it black with sugar? You keep going back to that food cart to give him your business because he's taken that extra step. He's made a mental note of your preferences and he's always ready with that steaming cup when he sees you coming around the corner. He lets you know that you matter. He's won a dollar a day in repeat business because he paid attention to you.

Someone who exemplifies this trait is my good friend Mike Kyser. Mike has built his career on relationship building. I remember the day he was hired. They gave him a phone and a desk and said you are now head of Crossover Radio. Make it work. Over twelve years he transformed into one of the best promotion guys in the business. He even acquired the nickname "the Mayor of Def Jam," and this year, because of his strong relationships and commitment to deliver, he was just announced "the Governor of Atlantic Records," a subsidiary of the Warner Music Group. Mike got connected and continues to build those kinds of relationships with radio, media and artists.

Our artists signed and stayed with us for that same reason. We've nurtured our relationships with them and put ourselves at their service. DMX is one of the most demanding artists in the business but at Def Jam he knew I had his back. When he dove into the audience and was mobbed by overeager fans, I dove in after him. I put his interests and safety before mine. In return, he performed!

Goodwill is golden. Do someone a good deed and it comes back, even if it doesn't always follow a straight line. Some people call it karma. I call it psychology. People want to feel respected. It's that simple.

It doesn't matter who that person is, or where they rank in your world. The goodwill has to flow up, down and sideways, because a bad turn can easily come around and bite you in the behind. In business, an intern can become president and end up being your boss. Your best friend can become your biggest professional rival by taking a job in a competing company. Today, Jay has my spot as president of Def Jam, and we're still great friends.

People move around a lot, especially in the music industry, so it's even more important to do right by others. Even though I was in shock after I left Def Jam, just a few weeks later L.A. Reid and I were having dinner together as friends. We've been making a point of meeting up for a meal once a month ever since. We are compatriots in an industry where African-American executives are all too few, we want to give each other all the love and support we can.

Whoever says success in business comes from being cut-throat and looking out for number one has it all twisted. You don't build a loyal following of people who can help you make it happen by being nasty.

Donald Trump says in his book *How to Get Rich* that if you've got them by the balls, their hearts and minds will follow. Respectfully, I disagree. When you have them by the heart, you control how much blood is pumping through the rest of the body.

My whole career has been about taking care of the needs of those below me, across from me and above me. I pour their coffee the way they like it. I put on the blue overalls and treat everyone as if they are my best customers. I give them service with a smile.

Report for Duty

A good friend of mine, radio deejay Frank Ski, once told me, "Always make the person you're negotiating with feel like they got the better deal."

Ultimately, you're still going to get what you want, even if you have to shave off a few percentage points, but that person is going to walk away thinking, "Damn, I really liked doing business with her. I'm going to come back to her with the next deal."

People like to feel their interests are part of the equation. Even in the supposedly cutthroat world of business, they like to know that you care about them as fellow human beings. To quote another Trumpism I happen to agree with this time, "Consider what the other side wants."

But I think you should go further and really *know* what the other side wants. You've got to switch yourself off so that you can really hear what they are saying and understand where they are coming from. When any type transaction is going down, you've got to *be present*.

This is true in any business situation. But in the hip-hop music world that I operate in, it's gospel. I am in the business of selling people who turn themselves inside out to make art. I'm dealing in precious human cargo that needs to be handled with care.

That's why, no matter how high in the corporate food chain I get, I'm always willing to carry that tray. I still wait on young artists who show up late for radio interviews. It's important, not just to let them know they matter, but to show the love and respect to the radio personalities and program directors who want to meet our artists.

It was service with a smile about two days before Thanksgiving 2004, when we were about to do a "Joint Chiefs" show at the Apollo in Harlem.

Every fourth quarter in the music industry, we do events like that to help promote our artists when they drop their big albums of the year. Atlantic Records is a unit of Warner Music Group and the Joint Chiefs are that label's major hip-hop artists: Fat Joe, T.I., Fabolous, Trick Daddy and Twista. This was going to be the landmark event of our multi-artist promotional campaign, with proceeds from the concert going to Hope Leadership Academy in Harlem, and charities in one of South Africa's poorest communities.

The event sounded great on the radio, but the timing was wack. The show was supposed to start at 7:00 p.m. No one realized that people aren't going to show up for a cool hip-hop event at that hour! By the time me and Julie Greenwald, the boss at Atlantic, got there at 6:30, there might have been 100 kids in a theater with a capacity of 1,100. Disaster!

Then and there we decided to push back the show until 8:00. I couldn't have my artists play for a half-empty auditorium, especially when they were doing a free concert for charity. They can't put their whole heart into their performance under those circumstances. So Julie and I worked 125th Street, walking the block from Champs Sports, which was sponsoring the event, to Foot Locker, Dr. Jay's, Jimmy Jazz and all the other spots where kids and their parents might be shopping before the holidays. I went into the record store on the corner and said, "Hey, y'all want to have your kids come in and see a free show, courtesy of Atlantic Records?"

People couldn't believe it. Most of the folks in that part of town know I'm Kevin Liles, a top music executive, and there I was shaking hands, introducing myself and personally inviting them to a concert. They said, "Yo, I'm going wherever you want me to go!" Soon I had a whole crowd following me down the street to the Apollo. Just before curtain time, that joint was full.

It didn't matter that I was some fancy corporate executive. The bigger cause was making that show so hot that the artists would feel great about the event we set up. We were ready, willing and able to do what had to be done. We were there to serve.

Wear Your Heart on Your Sleeve

Most rap artists in the hip-hop world don't give a damn about making it to their interviews on time. They don't like doing the work of marketing their albums. As soon as they sense that we are thinking about the bottom line more than their own personal needs, as soon as anyone makes the mistake of treating them more like commodities than human beings, we've lost the battle. If they think for a second that you're not feeling them, most of these guys won't even get out of bed for you if you beg them.

At Def Jam we always prided ourselves on making the artists know that we had them covered and that we always wanted what's best for them. A little extra effort and self-promotion can make the difference between an album going platinum or only selling 400,000, but the artist has to want it. It was our job to make the artist want it.

Few artists have tested me more than DMX. He's the real thing. He's come up from a life of poverty and crime to have one of the most enduring careers in hip-hop history. The fans love him because every time he performs he gives a piece of himself.

On Jay-Z's "Hard Knock" tour, a fifty-show, fifty-eight-day grind, X had a half-hour set. He was out there alone on the stage, rapping nonstop, with no hype man (part of the performer's crew who gets the audience worked up). He wanted to hit every single person in that audience with his rhymes, and he wanted to do it all by himself. What we didn't know at the time was that X was having a really bad asthma attack.

He came off the stage, dripping in sweat, and collapsed. We called an ambulance and they put him on a gurney, but then he heard Jay-Z out there singing "Money, Cash, Hos," a joint that features X, and X wasn't about to be left out of that one. He got up and we begged him not to perform. We were afraid he'd pass out. But he took one puff from his inhaler and rushed onto the stage with his trademark growl.

The audience was none the wiser that he was suffering. His voice already has a distinctive raspy quality that was even more so because he wasn't getting enough air! He gave the performance of a lifetime. X could have died that night. But once he's on, he's on. Somehow the rhymes kept coming out of him, even when he was running out of air.

X told me afterward he would have rapped to death. That's just the kind of artist he is. He'll do anything for his fans. I've been with him in the street when he's handed out fistfuls of hundred-dollar bills to complete strangers going through the struggle. The man is all heart.

One time in Miami, in a series of events that made us miss the last flight to London where he was supposed to give a concert the next day, he met a little girl who was selling candy so that she could go to camp. He asked her how many more boxes she had to sell. She said five. So X handed her five crisp hundred-dollar bills, took her mom aside and said, "This is for camp. Make sure you don't go shopping."

But dealing with X can also be a challenge.

That day in Miami, we were due to go to London for the MOBO Awards, which is basically the British version of the Soul Train Awards. It was our only spot on the show, and if we didn't show up, they probably weren't going to invite any Def Jam artists again. We took the huge risk of booking X, who'd already blown off two MTV awards shows, because we knew how much the English fans loved him.

X had an earlier event in Miami, so the plan was for us all to meet at the airport. Me and my homeboy, Keith "Cold Pepper" Parker, had our stuff loaded in the British Airways first-class cabin. We were in our seats when I got the call from Tony Austin, one of my A&R directors at the time, telling me they in were in the limo and on their way to the airport, but X didn't feel like going to London.

I flipped out. I said, "Tony, I don't care what X says, just get him on this plane so that he can tell me to my face he's not coming."

A few minutes later I got another call. "X isn't feeling well. He's sick. He wants to go to the hospital."

To this day I still don't know what was wrong with him. I figured he was faking, since a severe asthma attack didn't stop him from going onstage when he chose to, but what could I do? Deny a sick man medical attention?

Keith and I left the plane, which took off to London with all of our stuff, and headed to the hospital to see X. At his bedside I asked him, "X, you good? What do you need?"

X seemed fine, physically. I figured he was testing me. He was uneasy about going to London. He was just acting out. I had to be gentle, but firm.

"Please, I'll get you anything you want," I told him. "Just let's get back to the airport. We've got two hours to catch the last plane!"

The doctor was getting ready to discharge him. But X insisted he had a prescription to fill and that he had to do it then and there because he couldn't fill it in London. So off we went to find a Walgreen's with minutes ticking by until the next

British Airways flight. X got his meds and the last plane took off without us.

I decided we were going to be on the first morning flight out of Miami if it killed us. I got rooms in a hotel on top of the airport that night. I wasn't taking any chances. It wouldn't be the first time X would have gone AWOL and I wanted to keep a close eye on him.

I had Keith, who's a police officer in Baltimore when he's not helping me out, keep the night watch outside X's room. At six in the morning, knowing X would probably try to sneak out of the hotel, I set up my laptop and files in the downstairs lobby and kept my eye on the elevator door. Sure enough, out popped X at 7:30, trying to give us the slip before breakfast!

We made that morning flight to Heathrow. But the marathon still wasn't over. I'd booked him a silver Mercedes with a driver, but he saw my Range Rover and decided he wanted one too. We couldn't even leave Heathrow without having another scene, so I promised to get him a different car.

When we got into the city, X refused to go to the dress rehearsal. X considers it an insult to his art when he's asked to rehearse. But he had to go for safety reasons because there were going to be pyrotechnics in the show.

Keith and I still didn't have our luggage, which flew to London without us. Neither of us had slept in more than twenty-four hours and we were still in the same clothes. We'd have loved to go back to our hotel rooms, sleep and shower. But in the few hours to kill before the awards show, X wanted to visit a hobby store on Oxford Street. Of course, I had to go with him.

After about an hour of browsing, X bought himself a model plane. He wanted to go to Hyde Park to fly it, so I humored him. We had less than two hours to go before the show, but it was starting to look like I'd never be able to separate him from his new toy. He was having way too much fun in a park in the middle of London, miles from where we were supposed to be!

Soon we were attracting too much attention. Two policemen came up to us and asked X very politely to land the plane. That thing had a wingspan of at least eight feet. Anti-terrorist security measures after September 11 prohibited unauthorized flying objects in the city's parks, they explained.

But X just shrugged and said, "What do I know, I'm just a tourist."

Finally he crashed his plane into a big old chestnut tree. Instead of giving up the diversion, X climbed up the tree, retrieved the plane and started flying it. It wasn't until a little boy with his mother saw X and ran up to him to ask for his autograph that X landed his brand-new, $2,000 toy, signed one of the wings and gave it to the little boy.

There were a few more mishaps on the way to the concert that night. X kicked his driver out of the Range Rover we'd hired for him so he could drive through the streets of London himself. He also decided to take a nap just minutes before he was due to go onstage. X is almost narcoleptic. When that guy goes to sleep it's like he's in a coma. By some miracle we woke him up and, as usual, come showtime, X was on full-blown. The British fans went crazy for him!

Looking back, I realize now that X got on that plane and made that concert because I cared enough to see him in the hospital. I was worried about making that flight, but I showed enough concern about his condition. I took responsibility for his welfare. I stuck by his side in London, catering to his every need and hanging out with him to make sure he was okay.

I wore my heart on my sleeve. I showed interest in X as a human being, and therefore X delivered. To this day we love and respect each other. X is my brother.

The Power of Nice

I don't get mad. Rage is just negative energy to me.

Sure, I get irritated when someone drops the ball. I get annoyed in bad traffic. Once in a while I yell to make myself heard by my assistants down the hall. But I never let anger get the better of me. I refuse to lose control, no matter how much somebody tries to provoke me.

On rare occasions, you have to go there. If I see a roadblock I know I can bust through, and my sending that signal will make the other person realize, "Oh, he ain't playing," I will drive on through.

If I see someone who has the potential and should know better, repeating the same mistakes because they're just not getting the message, I let them know. If an artist constantly fails to show up to do radio interviews and doesn't do right by himself and the label, I'll give them hell. They know I do it because I care and I believe they can do better.

But when you do have to take it close to the edge, don't fall off the cliff. Go to an eight or a nine, but never a ten. Be the center of calm so that people can trust you not to overreact.

In the hip-hop world there are plenty of opportunities for people to go at it. The news is full of rappers beefing with each other. But that's overblown. It's the people who use their heads and stay cool who get the most respect.

Look at LL Cool J. True to his name, LL has the coolest head in the history of rapping. Whenever another artist started a beef with him, he never resorted to violent tactics. He'd keep his rivalry strictly on the artistic level, channeling it into his lyrics.

In 1987, Kool Moe Dee, feeling LL nipping at his heels, came out with the song "How Do You Like Me Now," dissing and taunting LL, the up-and-coming King of Queens. LL responded with "Jack the Ripper":

> How You Like Me Now punk? You living foul
> Here's what my game is, kill is what my aim is
> A washed up rapper needs a washer, my name is—
> Jack the Ripper . . .

LL's album went multiplatinum and Dee disappeared off the rapping scene for good. LL's still here, doing movies, putting out hot new albums and launching a clothing line, and no one had to get hurt. At least not physically.

When we did the Hard Knock tour, I had a misunderstanding with Damon Dash, the president of Roc-A-Fella Records and one of our partners. Roc-A-Fella artists were in the tour, but we made Def Jam jackets for everybody with their names embossed on each one. The rappers loved it, but Damon went ballistic.

He was pissed because he thought my small gesture meant that Def Jam was trying to take the credit for the tour. While his barber was shaving his head in the men's room backstage, Damon called me over. He could hardly sit still, he was screaming so much. "Are you f_____ foolish," he kept hollering.

Mostly I kept quiet. I tried a few calming words to placate him. I said, "Dame, Dame, calm down. They're just jackets." But he wasn't having any of it.

All this time a camera crew was around and this whole exchange went on tape for a documentary that was being made. I had the final say about what to cut, but I decided to keep the scene in. People said, "Kevin, you're crazy. Do you want people to see how that homeboy was playing you out?"

I wasn't worried. Like a friend told me not long after the scene went down, "When two people are in a room and one of them is screaming and waving his arms while the other one stays silent, who's the fool?"

People can get aggie with me. They can yell. They can curse.

As long as they don't hit me or threaten my family, I don't react. I know that when someone is that angry and crazy with rage it's not really about me.

People in the hip-hop culture have been through more pain than you could imagine. They've had to fight all their lives to get what they think is theirs. In their minds, they're still in the struggle. When they lash out, they're doing it for all the times they felt they got screwed. Whenever anyone loses it like that, they are suffering. It's their pain, not yours. Leave them to it.

My Little Black Book

Some guys just aren't worth going out on a limb for. In business and in life, there are relationships that are beyond redemption. For those I always keep an entry space free in a little black book.

That book doesn't exist anywhere but in the back of my head. I won't actually write the names down, nor will I ever reveal who's on the list. But I know exactly who's on it. Right now, the number stands at eighteen. The entries date all the way back to middle school, with the first time a white kid made a racist remark to me.

It takes a lot of negativity to land in my book. I can forgive a lot, but if someone does something with the intention of causing me or my family some kind of misfortune or harm, it's over. I will not have a relationship with that person beyond the bare necessity.

Even then, I won't respond to them in another negative way. Whoever makes my list will always be at the receiving end of plain old-fashioned good manners, no more, no less. I will never engage. If I see someone on my list in the hallway or on the street, I'll just say, "Hey, how are you doing," and walk on.

Kill Them with Kindness

I'm not an eye-for-an-eye kind of guy. I'm not mean. I like to keep my conscience clean. I believe in karma and kindness. Do unto others as you would have done unto you.

When you stay in a particular industry for a while, the same people keep circulating again and again as rivals, colleagues, bosses and friends. That's why it's always wise to invest enough time and thought into your business relationships to make sure that, whenever possible, everybody's straight with each other.

I'm no Pollyanna. I don't trust anybody. I keep meticulous notes and records of everything I do because I know that people are always going to try to get over. It's a dog-eat-dog world. But that's all the more reason why you shouldn't be that way. The less you are like the rest of the rats in the race, the more you will stand out. Even the biggest thugs will do right by you if they know you've got their backs, and if they don't do right otherwise, at least they won't shoot you!

I am living proof that you don't have to eat the other dog. The people I worked with at Def Jam became my biggest cheerleaders, even as I was jumping over them in the corporate hierarchy. I count Mike Kyser and Thomas Lytle, who worked with me as senior executives at Def Jam, among my most loyal friends. I was their junior, a kid from Baltimore who reported to them when they were running promotions. But I always helped them. I always served. If they ever begrudged my success while they were working under me, I never felt it.

My business relationship with Julie Greenwald has gone through all kinds of transformations over the years. But we've always been friends. She was the one who ultimately hired me to work for Def Jam in 1993. After I interviewed for the full-time position in New York City, she was the one who called me and said I got the job. They offered me $30,000 and I said, "Okay, I guess I can work with y'all for that."

There was a pause. Then Julie, who'd started at $18,000, got a little annoyed. She said, "No, you will work *for* us for that."

Julie was fierce. That baby girl put me in my place. But soon we became each other's best partners. We were the only ones staying behind in the office until midnight cooking up ideas for promotions, tours and albums. We used to sit in a room together and just get creative. We'd disagree with each other about stuff all the time, but by doing so we pushed each other toward greatness. Julie was my stand-up girl. She had my back.

She was running the promotions department when I was running the mid-Atlantic region and working on the Howard University homecoming event. I was given a budget of $1,500. It was a lot of money in those days, but I wanted to do it up right. I took out giant ads all over the D.C. area. I laid out $5,000 of my own money, unauthorized, but that homecoming and after-party will go down in Howard history as the hottest ever. Biggie and Method Man performed that year.

When the promotions people at Def Jam HQ found out how much I'd overspent, Julie got called in and screamed at. They were going to fire me!

The finance people refused to give me back my cash. Julie became the tiger once again. She went right up to Lyor Cohen's office and told him the situation. He wouldn't hear of it. He gave me my money back and praised us for a job well done.

I felt bad that Jules had to do the end-around on my behalf. Back then, some people were still gunning for me. The promotions department was skeptical of me and my big ideas. I was an outsider who came in to shake things up. I was aggressive. I wasn't showing off. I just wanted to do great things. But that doesn't always win you fans when people are just there to party and keep the status quo going.

Not Julie. When I thanked her once again for saving my ass and risking her own neck to help me get my money back, she just said, "Kevin, I love you. It was for a righteous cause."

We were both ambitious. We were both driven. When I made president, things could have changed between us. But she was always my sister. For a few months, while she was at Atlantic and I was at Def Jam, she was my direct competition. I'm so glad we're working as a team again under Warner Music Group. We have a relationship in business and in life that is built to last.

If you show everyone you encounter on your way to the top an unwavering level of respect and professional courtesy, whether it's the receptionist who answers the phone or the CEO, people will want to do business with you, again and again and again.

Know When to Edit

That doesn't mean all relationships are equal. Some associations are toxic. Others don't get you where you need to go in life. And some are so solid that they just don't need the same amount of time.

I love everybody, some more than others. But every now and then I have to edit certain friends and associates from my life. You have to constantly tweak and change how much to invest in your relationships. You have to decide when it's right to take a few steps back.

Ask yourself:

Who are the people around me who make me feel energized to make it happen?

Who's always telling me, "You can't?"

Who's a distraction?

Who knows when to leave me be and let me achieve my mission?

Who's happy for me when I succeed?

Who's always looking for something to criticize?

Who's being direct and honest in a supportive way?

Who's up my ass all the time?

Who has an agenda?

Who's along for the ride?

Who's not taking care of their own business?

Who's always interfering in mine?

Who's always ready to lend a helping hand?

Who's always got his hand out?

Who brings me up?

Who brings me down?

You'll be surprised what a relief it can be to edit some people from your life. You can go on for years doubting yourself, then realize that the source of that lousy self-esteem was a "best friend" who is always putting you down. Cut 'em loose and see how light and free you suddenly feel.

I'm not saying it's easy to edit your relationships. It's not even always necessary to put certain friendships on the chopping block. But the busier you get, the more fine-tuning needs to be done.

However invaluable your network may be, not every relationship carries the same currency. It's just a fact of life that as you evolve and you become more successful in your career, you will need to distance yourself from some people as you draw closer to others.

As a manager I have to be like the father who loves all his kids equally. But if I sense that someone is getting too dependent on me, I have to push them back a little. It all starts with, "Kevin, can I get a ride with you?" Now and then is okay. I'm a boss with an open-door policy. I like to vibe with everyone and help him or her as if they are friends, but when it's every day, it's got to stop.

If it's not a ride, it's an excuse. "Oh Kevin, sorry, I didn't call that program director. I've got so many other problems . . . I forgot . . . Can I have a raise . . ."

Before I know it, I've created an unhealthy dependency. They're in my office all time, bringing little decisions and problems that in their position they should be able to resolve themselves. They're sitting at my desk. They're using my phone. They're even using my executive bathroom!

A few times I let it slide. It's a fine line in any creative industry, where you keep the door and the communication channels open. I joke around with employees. We call each other names. It's all in fun.

But if it happens too often, I could find myself in a position where I'm getting played. It may not even be a conscious thing. It may not be manipulation. But when colleagues get too close their vision goes. They blur the lines between friend and employee. Familiarity breeds laziness. People start making assumptions.

I know if I'm seeing them all the time, their own work isn't getting done, and their department has lost its leadership.

You Can't Take Them *All* with You

I knew a lot of people back in the days when I was hustling. Growing up I had contacts sprinkled in all kinds of different crews. Dabbling kept things friendly. But I made a point of never getting in too deep.

These days, when I go back to Baltimore I see the same people on the same corner that I left fifteen years ago. Grown men with children to feed and no jobs and no future. Seeing them and stopping to talk to them keeps me grounded and helps me appreciate what I have.

Knowing how bad it is back home for so many people also inspires me to give back to their community so that their kids don't end up in the same place. I give my old associates money when they are in serious need and I happen to find out about it. Usually I give them a few minutes of my time when I bump into them and wish them well.

About three years ago I gave some of the guys on the corner Def Jam jackets. There were twenty jackets. When I'd drive past the old spots, I'd recognize them because they always wore their jackets. Recently I drove down Liberty Heights, doing the circuit past Sparky's Laundromat, the corner liquor store and the old 7-Eleven where we all used to hang.

Urban renewal seems to have missed that part of Baltimore. Houses and stores are boarded up. There are more homeless people, including some of my old friends. Doing the circuit, I could only spot four of the jackets. Two of the guys were killed, and two others are in jail. It made me sad.

I know some of my acquaintances are still in the game. A couple of years ago, an artist came to my hometown for a concert. Some of the guys from the corner approached my homeboys Rod and Tuffy and tried to convince them to take the artist to Liberty Heights and Gwynn Oaks so they could jump him and take him for all he had on him.

Rod said, "Come on, he's with Def Jam, that's Kevin's label. You can't do that to Kevin." They backed right off.

I'm still cool with everyone in the street because I made a tactful retreat. I don't run from anyone. I don't walk around with security. I don't avoid people because they are difficult or they've had a harder life than me. But as much as I want to take care of everyone, they can't all ride with me. There's just not enough room in the car.

That doesn't mean I won't give someone a chance when I know they've been in the game. When I see a guy I know has a lot of business sense, I don't run from him, whatever he's done. If he has hustle, he also has potential. But I won't do business with him without first removing him from his environment and crew. I have to create a safe environment where he can truly be himself.

The tragic flaw in most of these kids is their susceptibility to peer pressure. Nowhere is that worse than in a street gang. I've fallen under peer pressure to do stupid things. It's a negative. It's a desire that other people have to make you conform and keep you down. But I've probably influenced people more than I've been influenced.

If you are part of a group, be strong. Be your own person. Don't blame others for allowing yourself to get used or manipulated by your peers. If you allow yourself to be used, it means on some level you wanted to be exploited. Be accountable. There is such a thing as free will.

Over and over again I've seen artists' careers destroyed by hanging around with the same people they knew from their times of struggle in the street. Dozens of people who never wanted to know them back then now come along for the perks. Hustlers and gang members show up claiming you owe them a piece of the action. Resentment turns to violence and people get killed.

For many artists, surrounding yourself with the right crew is life and death. You can't bring the street all the way with you on the path to success. The rappers who survive know they have to keep that delicate balance between staying in touch and giving back to the community on the one hand and distancing themselves from all the sh__ that can go down on the other.

I have people I counted more as associates than as friends who were serious hustlers back in Baltimore. But I decided long ago to remove myself from their inner circle. I'd moved on to a new kind of hustle. If you want to be a millionaire, you should hang out with millionaires. If you want to be a billionaire, you should hang out with billionaires. There's nothing wrong with upping your game.

It's natural to want to hang out with your friends and bring them along to enjoy your success, but you have to make sure that their inappropriate behavior doesn't pull you back down with them.

The same goes for relatives. I'm an immediate-family sort of guy. I'm close to my parents and sisters, but my own kids come before anyone else. If my cousins, aunts, uncles, brother or birth father come to me continually with their hands out, I do what I can and then back off. If they are not at least attempting to do good for themselves and other people, it doesn't interest me to be around them. It's just negative energy to me.

True Crews

I travel with a small but select crew of friends. I make sure at least one or two of my homeboys from Baltimore come with me on business trips all the time. But we make sure that we don't become an unruly clique that excludes or intimidates other people. We operate on a strict code of behavior that's welcoming and respectful to others. When we travel to another person's house, we are model guests.

I'll be loyal to my homeboys from Baltimore forever. There are few people in this world I know will truly have my back. You have to treasure the people who knew you from back in the day. Me, Rod, Tuffy, Tuffy's brother Keith Parker, my cousin Tony and deejay Reggie Reg are tighter than most families.

They knew me when. We've been through life-and-death situations together. Our friends have been shot and killed. We've ducked bullets in the street. We developed a code of honor between us: don't knock each other's hustle. Even though I've come up in the world and I've got millions in my bank account, they don't ask me for a thing.

When I go home to Baltimore, my homeboys bring me back

down to earth. To them I'm still little Kev. I can be sitting in the finest restaurant in Baltimore and Tuffy will grab me in a friendly headlock. None of my friends or associates in the New York music world could get away with that!

I've always tried to keep at least one of my best friends from Baltimore with me in New York to help me keep it real and watch out for my interests. These days I keep my cousin Tony by my side. But Rod was the first to come.

Since our Numarx days, Rod wanted to get in the music industry. I wanted his company so I made him my driver. I thought if I kept him close enough to me and exposed him to enough of the inner workings of Def Jam, he might learn a few tricks and I could justify finding him a position doing A&R or promotions, or something.

For the first six months, Rod was full-blown into it. I told him I wanted him to be two weeks ahead of me in everything and sometimes he actually did take the trouble to anticipate my needs. I expected Rod to keep up with me in spite of my eighteen-hour days.

Maybe I was tougher on him because he was my friend and I didn't want to show too much favoritism. But Rod balked at the long hours. He'd drive me home and we used to argue like hell. "Kevin, when am I going to get a position? When are you going to pay me the real money?"

The hard work and sacrifice I expect from myself and the people under me just wasn't for Rod. He wanted to party. He told me he preferred the easy life. We had a blast together. But eventually it was Rod who recognized that he was in the wrong environment. He went back home to Baltimore and joined the fire department. I love him for that. His true vocation is helping people in need.

Tuffy took a break from his job as a fireman and replaced Rod as my driver. But again, like old times, we'd argue something chronic. Tuffy is stubborn and a maverick. I used to call up Rod and complain, "Tuffy is unmanageable!"

Tuffy didn't mind the hard work, but he hated the celebrity BS that comes with my job. He made a point of being unimpressed with some of the artists. He even picked fights with some of their crew. A diplomat he was not.

Tuffy was so protective of me that a couple of times I was afraid of what he would do when the CEO of one of our partner labels started disrespecting me in a meeting. In a way it was comforting to know Tuffy had my back like that.

Eventually, Tuffy left. He has a wife and family back in Baltimore and he missed his job putting out real fires. I didn't want either Tuffy or Rod to go. But at the time they knew better than I did that they would be better friends for me in the long term if they were allowed to live the lives they were meant to live back in their own environment.

I will never cut my homeboys from my life. I know they've got my back and I've got theirs.

The other day, my crew came into Baltimore for the day just to see me. I'd been traveling for weeks and I hadn't had the chance to be home. They came up to my office just to kick it with me for a couple of hours. But most of the time I was on the phone or in and out of meetings.

At the last minute a business dinner got cancelled, so I called my homeboy Rod to see where they were at. They'd been at a bar drinking since early afternoon and were getting in the mood to go grab some dinner, so I met them at the restaurant.

We had a great time reminiscing! My homeboys were pretty wasted by then, and we laughed and laughed like we always do. But in the hour and a half it took for dinner to be served and for me to eat and pay the bill, I was ready to go home, make some calls and unwind with a video game.

Rod said, "Kevin, I know how hard it was for you to sit still for an hour, so thank you so much for joining us for this long!"

He said it with love. They are true friends who know me well and accept me the way I am.

The same goes for my old friends from the KKK—Kevin Morton and Kenny Falcon. Kenny went into the security field. We might speak to each other once every three years or so. But our friendship is strong enough that our spirits can travel with each other.

As I've traveled the path to success, I don't look upon it as leaving my friends behind. I did what was best for me and my family. My closest friends are cheering for me. They were the first people I turned to for comfort when I left Def Jam. They only wish me the best.

When your crew is true, they're with you for life.

 **RULE 7**

What: Get Connected

Why: Build relationships to last forever because success in business depends on positive human interaction.

How: Keep an open mind and be compassionate. When you wear your heart on your sleeve, people bring you repeat business.

But: Don't be a doormat. Be selective about who you trust. When someone keeps bringing you down or telling you, "You can't," edit them from your life.

Rule 8

Step Outside Your Box: M.I.X.

Even other states come right and exact

It ain't where you're from, it's where you're at.

—Erik B and Rakim, "I Know You Got Soul"

As you come up in the corporate world, you're going to run into people from all cultures and walks of life. Business is the only true melting pot. Don't judge. Accept. It's on you to learn how to be a part of the mix.

Def Jam has become a global success because hip hop is for everyone. We started out as poor, black, urban culture because no one else would let us in. But now the rest of the world is knocking at hip hop's door and we're putting out the welcome mat.

Everyone has a culture or group that they identify with. Everyone learns traits and behavior from a cultural template. There's black urban culture, there's white suburban culture, there's culture based on race, religion, nationality, socioeconomic status, sexual preferences, age and interests.

It's human nature to want to latch on to a smaller community you feel comfortable with. From the time we're little kids we all want to dress and talk like that group in class we identify with the most.

But now it's time to shed some of those old clothes. Like the Reverend Al Sharpton said at last year's Democratic convention, "It's not about where you are coming from, but where you are going to."

Don't just be accepting of people from other cultures. Don't just ignore or tolerate. Go out of your way to form friendships and alliances with people you wouldn't normally encounter on your corner. Keep your own identity, but build an active social life that includes friends who are different from you.

Create a new culture that includes everyone of every color and community. Surround yourself with people who share your business values and work ethic, but who look, speak and dress differently from you. Understanding the markets of many by vibing with different people is the only way to blow up your success into something of worldwide significance. Why limit yourself by being exclusive to one community? Mix it up!

Some people call it diversity. Managers like to toss out employee numbers: 60 percent white, 20 percent African-American, 15 percent Hispanic, 5 percent Asian, 45 percent women . . . They worry about getting the right quota of race and gender. But those numbers don't mean sh__ unless you have a true blending of cultures and colors.

It isn't a numbers game. It's about the attitude. In hip hop, we're aiming for something bigger. We call it the "Browning of America."

Mixing it up isn't easy. We are living in one of the most

divided times in modern American history. We are faced with the greatest racial, class and generation gaps since the civil rights era. The poor are getting poorer and the rich are getting richer. People are laying blame on all sides.

It goes both ways. While I don't agree with everything Bill Cosby's been saying lately, he was right when he said that to play the victim of racism and talk about what the white man is doing against us "keeps you frozen in your hole that you are sitting in." We've got to own our stuff.

But he's wrong to sit in judgment against our culture. It's the hip-hop generation that's our best hope.

Our artists rap about life in the 'hood, but they are being heard by white kids in nice houses all over suburban America. Today, about 70 percent of CD sales go to middle-class white kids. These young men and women are identifying with each other from across the traditional social divides. White teenagers from Texas camp outside Def Jam's lobby door to work at a company they see as *their* cultural Mecca.

Hip-hop enterprises have Chinese, white, Hispanic, black, Jewish and Muslim employees working side by side toward a common goal. One of the great rappers of our time, Eminem, is white. That's not a new thing. The Beastie Boys—a bunch of white Jewish kids from Long Island—started out in the '80s.

Today we have Redman lookalikes in Japan. The British can't get enough of DMX and Jay-Z is vibing with Prince Charles. Kids in China rap in shopping malls about social freedom. Teenagers in the slums of Colombia rhyme about the oppression of violence from drug cartels and the military. Hip-hop disciples in South African shantytowns rap about poverty and AIDS.

Rap movements are taking hold right now in places I've never even heard of. Young people twenty thousand miles away from Hollis, Queens, have taken to our culture and adopted it as their own.

It's taken us three decades to get to this point. We still have our detractors, and we probably always will. Bill O'Reilly, the loudmouth on Fox Television, objects to the fact that white kids listen to black urban music. He rants about the swear words, even though there's plenty of profanity in predominantly white movies, video games, rock and punk music. You have to wonder why he's singling out rap artists.

He hates our culture so much that he uses his airtime on radio and on television to condemn rap artists like Ludacris. When Ludacris got a promotional deal with Pepsi in 2002, O'Reilly's calls for a boycott put pressure on Pepsi, and it immediately dropped the rap artist out of embarrassment and fear of hurt sales in middle America. Months later, Pepsi, helped by a backlash from African-American consumers, saw the light and renewed its ties to Ludacris. If it hadn't, it would have been a damn shame for many reasons, not least among them the fact that Ludacris is a philanthropist who donates a large part of his income to community groups and scholarships for underprivileged children through the Ludacris Foundation.

O'Reilly didn't mention that fact in his tirade. His ignorance and bigotry could have cost the very young people he claims to be trying to protect from hip-hop culture thousands of dollars in college funds. Now Pepsi is a major donor to the Ludacris Foundation.

O'Reilly is still trying to deprive rap artists of lucrative corporate sponsorships. But kids of all colors are a whole lot smarter than he is. They understand what our music is really about. When they listen to rap lyrics with swear words and a few descriptions of violence, they don't go out on a crime spree. They are sophisticated enough to realize that they are listening to a sound track that reflects the struggle against poverty. It makes them aware.

Don't Point the Finger

As hateful as these haters are, don't be like them. When O'Reilly wags his bony index finger in judgment, ignore it. You can make him, and his hysterics, irrelevant by handling your business and conducting yourself in a way that's accepting of all cultures and colors.

As a black executive, I bump up against prejudice all the time. I fly first-class to meetings every week, but I'm the only guy in first class who gets asked to show his ticket before taking his seat. It's funny to me. People should never judge a book by its cover.

It's easy to react to that kind of suspicious reaction. But if you give people a chance and talk to them, you'll be surprised. I know that as soon as I open my mouth, my friend in the aisle seat will get a sense of who I am and open up to me. I've learned a lot from my in-flight conversations with these other executives and they've learned a lot from me.

On a recent red-eye from New York to L.A., I got to talking with a businessman from Wisconsin who was launching a new company manufacturing airplane window shades that could open and shut with the push of a button. He was a regular air traveler and he got so tired of the blinds getting stuck when he tried to open and close them manually that he decided to come up with a solution. The business itself sounded boring to me, but I was fascinated to learn what kind of thought process led to that simple but profitable idea.

Flying back from Miami last year, I couldn't figure out why this one middle-aged white dude sitting next to a pretty young girl kept eyeballing me from across the aisle. I could have taken it two ways, but I decided to smile back at him and be approachable. Finally he came up to me and said, "Excuse me, but my daughter says you're somebody famous. Would you mind telling me who you are?"

No, I didn't mind. I told him I was no celebrity, but I explained that I was the president of a music label called Def Jam and described what I did for a living. It turns out he was an executive for a large manufacturing company in Iowa. It didn't surprise or upset me that he hadn't heard of my company. I appreciated the opportunity to educate the man.

What followed was a long conversation about hip hop and the significant way it's shaping the mind-set of the younger generation. We talked at length about how mainstream corporate America can harness the energy of our culture and market it to that growing demographic.

By the time the plane landed, I had a better idea of how a traditional businessman thinks about the marketplace, and he came away with an appreciation for a demographic he never really knew existed. As we deplaned, we thanked each other for the interesting conversation.

It would be easy to set up our own exclusive club after being shut out for so long, but if we did that we'd just be hurting ourselves. We'd be missing out on points of view that have helped our brand grow from local to global. We'd be deprived of the Japanese version of Wu Tang Clan!

In a way I was lucky. I learned how to integrate early on, when our school district was rezoned and they sent two hundred black kids from my neighborhood to Pikesville Middle School. We were thrown into it with eight hundred white kids we never would have hung out with were it not for the fact that we found ourselves in the same school. It was an opportunity many kids in urban America don't have these days.

Sure there were tensions, but to this day I think that experience has taught me how to be accepting of others, no matter how different they are from myself. Pikesville gave me my first taste of racism, but it also showed me how people can overcome bias when they are forced to come together. Today, my son plays youth soccer with kids of all races on the very same field we used in middle school. It makes me feel like we laid the groundwork of integration for the next generation.

I learned a lot about how wealthy and middle-class suburban white kids speak to their parents. I remember being shocked by one kid who was giving lip back to his mother about something and said, "What the hell, Mom, that's stupid."

I don't know what shocked me more, the fact that he dissed his mother or the fact that he got away with it. My mother would have slapped me upside the head and grounded me for a month. I also met plenty of white kids who were poorer than me and a lot of the black kids I knew, who had no family stability whatsoever. It was like their parents just didn't care.

Not only did these early revelations make me realize who I was, they gave me a greater understanding of where these kids are coming from. It taught me not to knock their hustle. Everyone has their own strategy for survival and getting on in their life. Realizing this breeds tolerance. We need more of that in business and in life.

Respect

The only way to get respect is to show respect. When you're in someone else's place of business, you should conform to their rules. You don't go to other people's houses and walk across their brand-new carpet with muddy shoes!

I always travel with a small crew of friends who I trust to be welcoming to others and behave appropriately at all times. But our industry is full of entourages that are out of control. Their loud antics intimidate and antagonize other people, and hurt the way business goes down.

This happened on the set of Montell Jordan's video shoot, "Something for the Honeys," in 1996. Lyor had the brilliant idea of having rappers playing golf. A ghetto golf tournament! Now that was a place hip hop had never gone before!

We spent hundreds of thousands of dollars on the production of this thing. It took weeks of negotiation to persuade the managers of this exclusive billionaire golf club just outside of Los Angeles to let us shoot the video. We did not disclose that we were an urban music label.

This was in the mid-'90s, in the middle of all those beefs. Our image with people less familiar and less accepting of hip hop was a bad one. The managers would never have let us in. They'd have been too scared that our artists would trash the place and beat up their members.

But this was our big chance to show those people that we knew how to conduct ourselves and mix with groups of people culturally different from our own. While we don't conform in hip hop and we are proud of who we are, it makes no business sense to isolate ourselves from the mainstream. When we are in someone else's environment, we need to show that we can adapt.

We had everyone on that shoot set. We brought in two hundred scantily clad babes from L.A. as extras. Red and Meth, Snoop and the Dogg Pound, Coolio, all these people showed up. I can't remember who started it, but a person from someone's entourage had a beef with the members of the Dogg Pound, and all hell broke loose.

Everyone jumped into the fight. Golf carts crashed, golf balls were flung, bottles were broken. One of the guys in the middle of the beef took a golf club and hit his adversary over the head with it. Soon, the club's undercover cops were on the scene, pulling their guns out. Of course, we were kicked out of the club.

It was a mess. While no one on the Def Jam side was involved in the fighting, we lost control. Other people's crews, and the entourages of people who had nothing to do with the filming of the video, tore up the green and threw the first punches.

But it made us look bad. I had to go into damage control and sweet-talk the managers into letting us back in to do a reshoot. On top of the thousands of dollars we lost on the video, we had to pay several more thousand dollars in damages. I made sure I was there in person the next time.

When you're dealing with artists and the creative process, it's not always possible to control the mayhem. But as an executive in the music industry, I make a point of being proper and corporate in the way I conduct myself with people from other industries. It's how I represent.

Making people outside of your culture feel comfortable is critical to the success of any deal. Def Jam as a brand has expanded its reach into so many areas of the consumer and entertainment business—areas far removed from the hip-hop world—because of our ability to communicate and find the common ground with people unlike ourselves.

Take, for example, our deal with Electronic Arts, the biggest electronic gaming company in the world.

EA is known for its clean, family image. The company has become a multibillion-dollar business without resorting to the violence and profanity of its competitors' content because its products are so good. I've been addicted to Madden Football, the best-selling video game in the world, for years. I love it so much that I play it with my six-year-old son, Kevin Jr.

So three years ago, when I first heard that Larry Probst, the CEO of Electronic Arts, was looking to do business with the music industry, I was excited. It turns out that Larry had his eye on us for a long time. Contrary to appearances—one reporter compared Larry's demeanor to that of Defense Secretary Donald Rumsfeld, a comparison Larry was none too pleased about—this guy had his finger on the pulse of youth culture.

Larry was well aware of the importance of hip hop, and he was eager to attract more of the market that appreciates rap music by integrating some of our artists into his games. He told me he wanted to use our music and artists to make his games more compelling. I had more of a partnership in mind.

Before our meeting, I made a point of studying Larry and looking up his bio and news clips on the Internet. By learning where his head was, I could understand what his priorities were and find common interests to talk about to put him at ease.

My research taught me that he's a no-nonsense kind of guy who likes to get to the point. I liked that. I found out where he likes to vacation, what he likes to read, and what video games he likes to play (*Fight Night*). I learned that he's a golf fan and likes wine.

His business come-up took place in the most traditional of industries, working for the packaged goods business, moving on to Johnson & Johnson and Clorox. But he took a risk and left the security of that corporate world to be on the cutting edge of gaming in 1984.

A Google search helped me find out how his business was doing. EA had 22 percent of the North American market for video games and 60 percent of the sports games market, with sales of more than $2 billion. Everything they touched, it seemed, turned to platinum, with twenty-seven titles selling more than $1 million each.

By pushing up his market share just a few more percentage points to 30 percent, he could hit sales of at least $9 million. If he could work with us and push the envelope on content just a little more than usual, we could help him score some of that new market share.

Larry drove in from Redwood City to our offices in L.A. for the meeting with me and Lyor Cohen. His limo dropped him off in front of the Hustler Building on Sunset in Hollywood, where Def Jam's West Coast headquarters are located. By the time he walked past some X-rated window displays and up the stairs to Def Jam, he knew he was in for something different.

We were ready for him. We talked a lot about his business. I challenged anyone on his staff for any money to a game of Madden Football. Larry told me he wanted to use our artists and our music to create games with a more urban theme.

By being a gamer myself and researching EA's mission, we were able to change the rules of the traditional licensing of music. I suggested that we could do more to create synergy between EA, Def Jam and hip-hop culture. We struck a deal to make *Def Jam Vendetta*, the first hip-hop video game in history. In less than a year, it went platinum, and we started work on our next game, *Def Jam Fight for New York,* which was released in September 2004.

My efforts to understand Larry, and Larry's interest in our culture, enabled us to do business together. With us the name of the game was compromise from day one. By compromise, I don't mean in the negative sense of giving up your principles. I mean we negotiated our territory in a way that would be of mutual benefit. We met somewhere in the middle.

At first Larry was uneasy with some of our language and content. Video games get rated E for everyone, T for teen, M for mature and AO for adults only. About 15 percent of the market is M-rated, but Larry has long been reluctant to go there. I had to push him on the outer limits of a T rating.

We wouldn't let up. There had to be some slang if we were going to be true to our culture. Larry said, "Kevin, we are stretched to the furthest level we are comfortable with, but I understand your need for authenticity."

The next game we did was M-rated.

Watch Your Language

The best way to create a comfort level for others outside your culture is through the way you speak. When you make an effort to be understood by speaking plainly and avoiding slang and profanity, you are showing a desire to communicate clearly. Make it simple for them. Let them feel you. Put out the verbal welcome mat.

I don't have to wear a suit to be professional. As soon as I open my mouth, people can sense what I am about. But what they don't realize is that I am making a constant, conscious effort to adapt my language in a way that's appropriate to each situation.

I clean it up completely when I'm doing business with Larry, or putting together deals with the folks at American Greetings, or going to Arkansas to visit with Wal-Mart executives.

But speaking the hip-hop lingo is innate to me. It's the slang I grew up with. Every day, when I'm dealing with other people in the music business, it's natural for me to lace my conversations with the language of the street. I turn it up a notch when I'm dealing with artists, because that's how we get down.

It gets so bad that when I'm visiting my parents in Baltimore, I have to walk outside the house to conduct my phone conversations with other people in the music business. I'm dropping the F-bomb left and right. I may be thirty-seven years old, but that kind of talk under my mother's roof could still get me trouble.

Lately I've been thinking a lot about the power of language, especially the N-word.

When Bill Cosby complained last year about its common usage in our culture, it wasn't the first time I'd heard that. Use of the word has been discussed and disapproved of by the older generation for years. The older I get, the more torn I am about using it at all.

I can understand how the civil rights generation must feel about the N-word. It's offensive to them because they grew up in a time of segregation. I'm conscious of what our fore-fathers went through, and how the word was hurled at them by white folks trying to keep them down. To them, the word is de-meaning.

But for my people and my generation, it's become a term of endearment. I don't know how that happened. It just did. Some-how, growing up in an urban environment in the post–civil rights era, we took ownership of it. Today it's being peppered about in rap songs, movies, television and daily conversation almost like punctuation marks.

These days, the N-word is overdone. The word has gone from street to commercial. The wrong people are using it, even if they don't intend it to be heard as a racial epithet.

I would not insult my parents, or Bill Cosby, or anyone who came up during the civil rights struggle by consciously using the N-word. I certainly won't use it in conversation with white people and you won't hear me say it in my own home. I won't even spell it out in this book.

At the same time, I accept that other people use it and I don't judge. It's a part of the street language and culture I grew up in. But as I've matured in both life and business, I'm choosing to find better words.

Rise Above

Discrimination, in all its forms—white against black, black against white, men against women, rich against poor—is a fact of life. It's never going to disappear. You don't have to accept it and you certainly don't have to take it. But you can rise above it.

Joe Haskins, the chairman of Harbor Bank in Baltimore, is part of that generation of African-Americans who always had to fight for their rights. When he graduated from college in the 1970s, he wanted to go into finance, but back then there were even fewer men or women of color to be found on Wall Street.

Joe went through all the necessary steps, and then some, to get to where he wanted to go. He got his MBA, his MA, his advanced business degree. He had diplomas coming out of his ass. But when he graduated among the top five from a management training program at Chemical Bank, now J.P. Morgan Chase, he didn't get the premium positions. With his qualifications, he should have had his pick.

Instead, the bank flipped him around from one less desirable position to another. Over the next five years, he worked in internal audit. He did a stint in the factory unit. He put in time on the marketing side. What he really wanted was a coveted position in lending and investment, but he was told to wait until the bank's management was more comfortable with the idea of an African-American executive in a lending position. They just weren't used to the idea.

At the time, Joe resented getting bumped around. But he gutted it out and today he's even grateful.

"Sometimes what appears to be just a total disrespect or put-down can oftentimes have laced in it a richer or better experience," Joe says now. "I'm a better banker today because of my broader experience."

Serving so many functions on Wall Street gave him the tools he needed to start his own, very profitable, bank—one that is mostly staffed by African-Americans and makes loans to ethnic minorities who are usually turned down by the bigger institutions.

Don't Knock the Hustle

We had giant clashes of culture and personality at Def Jam. The label's female executives have a lot to put up with. Artists can be assholes. But unless your personal safety or livelihood is threatened, I don't recommend running off to complain to human resources about every little slight.

In any industry, this kind of conflict is inevitable. Men are pigs on Wall Street too. In the real world of business, you have to find a way to deal with it. You can't make other people go away. But you can come to a mutual understanding. Conflict is almost always resolved when somebody makes a sincere effort to appreciate the other person's hustle.

Gabby, Def Jam's video promotions director, and one of our artists come from opposite worlds. Gabby's an old-fashioned Italian-American girl from upstate New York who is all about business. The artist grew up poor, got into trouble, hustled and broke a few laws. He has an artistic temperament, and the lingering mind-set of a hustler trying to survive in the streets.

The result was a clash of personalities. Those two just couldn't mix it up. She turned into the ice queen when he was around, and he made a sport out of making her life difficult.

But they still had to work together. He is one of Def Jam's most important artists, and the media outlets all want him. It was Gabby's job to deal with those media outlets, set up television appearances, and handle the artists.

It all came to a head when she had to get him to show up for rehearsal for *Saturday Night Live*.

The artist is notorious for not showing up. He's tested the patience of every media outlet there is.

Lorne Michaels is well known in the industry for cancelling on performers who don't show up for rehearsal. He was scheduled for four full rehearsals in two days. To make sure he'd show up, Gabby put him up at the Marriott Hotel, a dog-friendly place where he could hang out around the corner from the NBC studios.

All she had to do was wake him up and get him to his first rehearsal on Friday morning. But right before the eleven o'clock appointment, he wouldn't wake up. His assistants shook him and got him to lift his head an inch off the pillow, but he just said, "I don't give a f___. I'm tired. I'm not going." Then he went back to sleep.

Gabby called Lyor to apprise him of the situation. Lyor flipped. He told her her job was on the line, and hung up. She negotiated with her contacts at the *SNL* set and got the morning rehearsal cancelled. All he had to do was show up at 6:00 p.m. and walk through the building to show Lorne his intention to be there the next day.

But a long night of partying and drinking with his crew put him in a deep sleep. He was out stone cold. All his boys were in the room with him, trying to shake him and wake him up, but just minutes before six o'clock it was clear he wasn't getting up for his walk-through. He was only being asked to reassure the nice folks at *SNL* that they didn't promo him just to be humiliated at showtime, but he didn't care.

Tired of waiting outside the man's hotel room door all day, Gabby barged in and screamed at him to get up. At 6:30, he came to, miserable and ready to throw a punch at somebody and growling that he wanted a bowl of Captain Crunch with milk and ice.

He told Gabby, "I don't have to do sh__. I don't give a f___ if they cancel my performance. If they don't believe I will be there tomorrow, then f___ them, how about that? They don't deserve my performance anyway!"

Realizing she had nothing to lose, all the years of frustration from dealing with him spilled forth:

"You always f___ up my sh__ and make me look bad! Not everyone else. Just me! I'm always lying for you, saying your wife's having a baby even when she's not pregnant, because every time I set something up, you act up. You're screwing with my relationships. What if every time you had a studio session and you needed to make a record I came in with a baseball bat and smashed up all the equipment so you couldn't record? What would you do?"

"I would punch you in the face," he said.

"Right," Gabby said. "That's what you make me want to do. I want to punch you in the face because you are always making me look bad."

Gabby got his attention. She reminded him that the poor kids in the ghetto he's always talking about couldn't afford the $55 it would cost to see him live at a concert, but they could watch him on *SNL*, even if they didn't have cable.

Then she delivered the final blow. "Forget that sh__ about doing it for your fans," she said. "You're not doing anything for anyone but your selfish self right now!"

Gabby walked out of the room in a big huff and headed toward the elevator, figuring her career was over. Then a colleague ran after her to tell her that he was up and getting dressed. He'd be in the building by 7:00 p.m. Lorne Michaels saw his face, and the show went like clockwork the next day, even without the rehearsal.

The artist didn't say anything to Gabby, but there hasn't been any trouble since. Gabby later came to realize that he was behaving that way because he felt that she, as a music executive, just saw him as a commodity and not as a person.

He asked her why she stopped speaking to him and acted like she didn't know him. He didn't get that she was personally hurt and upset that he made her look crazy in front of her counterparts at the media outlets she had to deal with on a daily basis.

Gabby realized something that day. "When I put it in human terms and made him see how I felt by breaking it down in a way so that he could relate, it worked," she said.

Those two will never be best friends. They're just too different. But they came to respect each other's hustle.

RULE 8

What: Step Outside Your Box: M.I.X.

Why: It will help you blow up your ideas to a global level. You have to be open to people from all walks of life because business is the only true melting pot.

How: Go beyond acceptance and reach out to people who are different from you. If they share your values and work ethic, it doesn't matter what they wear, where they are from or what color their skin is.

But: Don't lose yourself altogether. You can still do you, as long as you don't knock anyone else's hustle.

Don't Let Cash Rule

It seems we living the American dream

But the people highest up got the lowest self-esteem

The prettiest people do the ugliest things

For the road to riches and the diamond ring . . .

—Kanye West, "All Falls Down"

You can be rich and still think and act like you are poor.

Some of the poorest people in life own their own businesses and make millions of dollars a year. They're always worrying about losing it all and hustling to get the next dollar. They're looking out for number one, as if they still have to survive in the streets. The more you think that way, the greater the risk that greed will trip you up and send you right back where you started.

Others get rich quick and then lose their minds. They're spending for today and not planning for tomorrow. They're so excited about suddenly having the money that they get caught up in all the trappings they think they can afford. They blow it all on bougie status symbols that leave them feeling empty later on.

I can name you dozens of rappers who came up too fast from the ghetto and have suffered this fate. They have all this money before they know how to manage it. They're wearing their wealth around their necks in gold ropes and diamond chains. They're buying the Cristal and the pimped-up Escalades like the world is going to end tomorrow.

Most of them end up right back in the street with nothing to show for it. By the time they turn thirty the private planes are nothing but a dim memory.

I'm not saying money doesn't matter. I've loved the smell and feel of cash money in my pocket from the first time I had it. That's why I've had jobs since I was eleven. Even today, despite the fact that I have credit cards and bank accounts, I like to have a fat roll of bills in my pocket. Just knowing it's there gives me a warm glow.

But the first rule of wealth management is to understand that it's *not* all about the Benjamins. You've got to realize from the time you earn or steal your first dollar that true wealth is not about the money for money's sake or the flash of a diamond-encrusted watch.

Real financial success comes when you work hard and you earn cash for the long-term security it can offer you, your children and your children's children. You buy yourself the time and comfort level you need to sustain the balance between career and family. You create the wealth that keeps on creating, through investments, enterprise and philanthropy. You raise yourself up so that you can uplift the community.

Don't let the chase for dollars bankrupt your soul. That's not true wealth. Do like the Citibank ad says: "Live richly."

Horizontal Money

It's never too early to think about investing and managing your savings to give you choices in the future. As you build your own business or make your way up the corporate food chain, you should be taking steps toward financial security. It gives you the option to take risks without compromising your welfare.

It's tragic how little we know about wealth management in our culture. I wish everyone would learn the basics of accounting. It's our greatest weakness. If we learn the art of saving and having horizontal income, where you're laying down while your money makes money for you, we'll be a wealthier and more stable community because of it.

Because they grew up poor, most of these kids haven't had a parent or mentor to teach them about money. Most of them grew up in hand-to-mouth households where the bank was the loan shark on the corner. So many kids from our culture don't even know how to write a check. When you're born poor, you stay poor unless you make it your business to study up on the fundamentals of financial management.

I don't even have the excuse of growing up without true people close to me. My mother was an accountant. All those years I was rapping she begged me to set something aside!

It kills me to think about the wads of cash I flushed away on stupid stuff when I was first starting out in the music business. When I was with my rap group, we used to spend thousands of dollars on hotel rooms and rides, just because. As teenagers, spending freely was our expression of freedom.

Me, Rod, Tuffy and my other homeboys would stay in hotels less than a mile away from our parents' houses so that we could party and have our girl groupies over. We'd spend thousands buying the latest sound system equipment and call it investing in ourselves, even though we didn't always need it.

Back then, success to us looked like a big Benz, some girls and $3,000 in our pockets. Every cent we made as Numarx we pissed away like water. If I'd listened to my mother and invested some of those royalty checks, I might have had enough extra from those days to buy myself a six-room villa in the Caribbean.

Today I don't show my wealth. I have some hefty spending habits. I buy $30,000 watches for my friends. I go on first-class vacations to Capri and Monte Carlo. I've got a nice house in New Jersey. I bought my parents a big house in Baltimore. I have the standard executive black Mercedes and a black Range Rover, free of the fancy rims and trimmings. I'm an inconspicuous consumer who lives large.

But no matter how much I spend, I have savings and investments all over the place that I never, ever touch. I still keep a 401(k), and I've just written a will to make sure my children and my children's children are more than good.

You don't need to have millions to do this. It goes back to what my father once said: "Son, it's not how much you are making, but what you do with what you have."

I first sought financial advice when I was nineteen, after Numarx won the case against Milli Vanilli over the rights to our song "Girl You Know It's True" and the serious royalty checks started coming in. By that time I realized I had been losing too much money. We fought so hard, hiring lawyers and putting it on the line to get what was ours, that I realized I'd better try to hang on to my dollars.

The first trick I learned was to sock the maximum amount of income I could deduct into 401(k)s. When I got my job at World Connections Travel, I had them take 10 percent out of my paycheck. Before I knew it I'd saved up $47,000.

What you don't see, you're not going to spend. It's that simple. Because I never got that 10 percent of my salary, I never missed it. That money would be long gone by now if I'd had access to it. I'd get to a point where I'd have $20,000 in the bank and I'd say to myself, "Let me go buy myself something. Let me go and get myself a nice new ride."

I'm not going to give you all the answers to financial management in this book. But please, please, if you don't understand the basics of finance, take an accounting class, go online or read a book on wealth management.

I recommend *Rich Dad, Poor Dad*. That book taught me the difference between being rich and being wealthy. When I made my first million, I realized that it was just a step along the way to true financial well-being. It helped me decide to buy my first house instead of a lot of new toys.

Whatever you do, follow my instructions in the third chapter and GET EDUCATED! Even if you can afford to hire an accountant, never trust someone so completely with what's yours that you leave that person with all the power to make decisions.

If you can, find a close relative who knows accounting and who you can trust with your estate. If one of my nieces or nephews decides to study money management, I will pay for their education. There is nothing I would like better than to keep it in the family.

Slick Rick

There will probably always be conspicuous consumption in the rap world. You can't blame people who've been have-nots all their lives for wanting to celebrate their newfound state of having. For them, the latest watch or car is just another expression of empowerment.

But there's been a backlash lately. As the culture matures, older rap artists are beginning to understand the futility of owning all that stuff. Kanye West sums up our culture's conflict with consumerism in his song "All Falls Down":

> We buy our way out of jail, but we can't buy freedom
> We'll buy a lot of clothes when we don't really need 'em
> Things we buy to cover up what's inside
> Cause they made us hate ourself and love they wealth
> That's why shorty's hollering "where the ballas' at?"
> Drug dealer buy Jordans, crackhead buy crack
> And the white man get paid off of all a dat
> But I ain't even gon act holier than thou
> Cause f___ it, I went to Jacob with 25 thou
> Before I had a house and I'd do it again
> Cause I wanna be on *106 and Park* pushing a Benz
> I wanna act ballerific like it's all terrific
> I got a couple past due bills, I won't get specific
> I got a problem with spending before I get it
> We all self-conscious I'm just the first to admit it.

That's exactly what I'm talking about. The need to show our wealth on our sleeve could be our greatest downfall. Our culture is feeling the pressure to go out and buy status symbols before we even have the money in our hands.

The hip-hop industry has generated billions of dollars with the sale of records and consumer products from clothing to Pepsi. But how many of us do you see on lists like Forbes' 400 wealthiest? Too few to count, because we lack assets. Our showy displays don't just make us targets for muggings or shootings. We are hurting our long-term financial health.

I beg artists not to buy that new Bentley. Every day I'm watching people say to each other, "Yo, I bought this chain." I want to hear them say, "Hey, I bought this house," or, "I'm rebuilding this project and renting out ten different apartments."

There are a couple of rappers who understand the concept of investing. Slick Rick the Ruler is one. The man owns and manages three residential properties in the Bronx where he grew up. Today he lives very comfortably off the income.

Slick invented the gold-dipped style that so many artists have taken to. In the mid-'80s, when other artists were wearing sweats, he was the flossiest, stepping out in fur coats, velvet suits, silk shirts, gold and diamond grills and gator shoes. One of his best rhymes still makes me laugh:

> And when I smiled—BING!—I almost blinded her
> She said, "Great Scott, are you a thief
> Seems like you have a mouth full of gold teeth . . .

But no matter how many gold chains he wore around his neck, Slick, a Jamaican Brit, understood that the cornerstone of American wealth is in property. In many ways, having that solid, brick-and-mortar investment helped saved his life.

Like so many artists who find themselves with a lot of fast cash, Slick got to feeling like people were after his money. The sudden fame and wealth was messing with his head. He started carrying a piece. Then, in 1990, he got involved in a dispute over a potential robbery. He opened fire, people got shot and he landed himself in prison in upstate New York for five years.

After serving his sentence, the last thing Slick wanted to do was make rap albums. But at least he had his property and his family to go back to. Having that gave him a new lease on life and bought him the time he needed to get his head together before relaunching his career as a rap artist. Who knows what would have happened to Slick and his family if he didn't have his investments to fall back on?

Even if you don't want to invest in buildings, stocks or bonds, at least set aside enough for a rainy day. I never could have foreseen a time when I might be unemployed. But it happens to all of us, especially in the music business.

Doug Morris, Universal Music boss, worked his way up from the bottom and ended up running Warner's record label. But Time Inc. bought out the company, and Doug was fired the same day.

"The next thing I know, they cut off my cell phone and everything else, and I'm looking for lunch from a food vendor on Broadway," Doug said. "One day you're a CEO and the next day you're on the street buying a ham sandwich."

When I left Def Jam, money was the least of my worries. I knew that no matter how long I took to decide my best move, I'd be able to pay my bills and support my family. That security bought me the time I needed to sit by the pool in my backyard and reflect. I even had the wherewithal to take a vacation! Years of careful financial management gave me the power to choose what was best for my career without having to compromise for my next paycheck.

Pro athletes have even less job security than people do in the music business. But, at just twenty-five, NFL star Roy Williams is already wise enough to realize his time as a pro athlete is fleeting. He's working ahead to expand his options by networking with successful businesspeople, learning how they create wealth. Like I keep saying, if you want to be a billionaire, hang around billionaires.

Roy's worth a few million, but as he told me once, "Kevin, I'm rich, but I'm not wealthy." To those who haven't reached his income bracket, that might sound crazy, but I understand what he means. Roy hasn't made the critical mass of money that begets more money, at least not for the long-term future he envisions for himself and his family.

That's what he's aiming for by seeking professional financial advice, following the stock market and reading newspapers like the *Wall Street Journal*. He wants to retire his parents and make sure his sister, a single mom, is straight. He wants to have enough of a financial cushion that he can afford to continue to give money away to the causes he cares about without diminishing his own nest egg. That makes him a role model for our culture.

Create Wealth

Our grandparents' generation fought for the right. Our parents' sought the education. Members of our generation are becoming entrepreneurs and making the money. It's up to our children to create the wealth that keeps on creating. But it starts with us. We have to learn the art of money and lead the next generation in taking it to a whole new level.

Michael Lee-Chin has already done that. The Jamaican-born, Canadian fund manager controls assets he built up from $1 million to more than $11 billion. Not only is he one of the richest African-American men in the world, he's one of the richest men in the world, period. Few people know more about investing and creating wealth than he does. That's why more people from our culture should study up on this man to find out who he is and how he does what he does.

The opportunity to meet him came my way this past New Year's Eve in St. Barts. A few of us rang in the hour at an annual party on Ron Perelman's yacht. (And if you don't know who he is, GET EDUCATED! He took over Revlon and he's one of America's hundred richest men.)

The party continued all night, but a few of us, including Star Jones and her husband, decided to leave. As we walked along the harbor front, Star bumped into a girlfriend of hers who works with Michael. She said he wanted to meet us and invited us to come on up to his boat.

I got to spend the better part of the first morning of 2005 talking to the self-made man whose motto is "Buy. Hold. And Prosper." Talk about starting the New Year right! Michael encourages investors to create a strong, rational basis for their financial decisions and to never let emotions get in the way. He believes that America's richest got that way by owning at least one or two businesses. His philosophy for investment is to buy a few excellent businesses and hold onto them for the long term. It's a strategy that helps them build up their capital and keep it.

"You can't be an investor unless you think like a business-man. And you can't be a good businessman unless you think like an investor."

He didn't come up with these principles all by himself. Michael studied up on role models like Warren Buffett, finan-cial guru to the gurus. Now go read *Forbes* magazine and study up on Michael Lee-Chin.

Keep a Tab

There's an old saying, "Neither a borrower nor a lender be." But that's too hard. As soon as you start making the real money, people are going to hit you up for a loan. It's just a fact of life.

I'd rather be a lender than a borrower. When you ask some-one to lend you money, you're risking compromise, especially in the business world. Even when you've paid off that loan, there's always someone who constantly reminds you that they did you that favor. Who's to say you won't be pressured into doing something that goes against your principles?

There are few greater disadvantages in life than feeling like you owe someone. Of course, at the start of your come-up, you might find you need a little seed money. I borrowed cash from my parents when I was in my band. But make sure that paying it back is your first priority. And if you must borrow, at least make sure it's from a close family member you can trust.

It's hard to turn people down when they ask you for help. I'm not advocating that you deny your friends and family the occasional favor. But be as selective about who you would lend money to as you would be about what you invest in.

Make sure that person is either deserving, in genuine need or at least good for it. Make sure that your money, which you will probably never see again, is going to a valuable cause. But never lend more than you are prepared to lose.

I've been lending since I was in my teens and everybody around me knew I was making money. I was probably watching too many movies about the mafia, but, like I said before, I even started charging 10 percent interest on my lunchroom loans in school.

That was just a childish game. I haven't charged interest since then. It's hard enough to get back the principal and, unless you're a bank, that's not the right reason to give someone a loan. You do it because some people are less fortunate. I'm not trying to heal the world, but I want to help people achieve some things in life that are positive.

I've lent thousands of dollars to friends and associates. I've helped people pay their expenses when their car breaks down, or when they've gotten themselves into a debt hole and can't feed the family. I've even lent money for the down payments on houses.

But even if I know deep down in my heart that I will never see that money again, I keep a running tab. I've had as much as $500,000 loaned out to various people. The tab reminds me not to loan money to the same person twice if they never paid me back.

I haven't always lent money to the right people for the right reasons. When I was sixteen years old I spotted seven Gs to one of my street friends. It was a lot of money to me back then. We were doing a hustle together and we had to invest in some product. A few days later he came back to me and said, "Kevin, my house got robbed, I can't pay you back."

Even if his house caught fire, that's not the issue. If I give someone $7,000 and they say they are going to get it back to me, they are responsible for that money.

Two years ago I lost $10,000 to Jay-Z in a Guts card game. I sent a check over to his studio by messenger. But he wanted to be paid in cash. He sent the check back with a message for me: "Tell Kevin to come and pay me in person." He was right. It's about meeting your obligations. When you owe someone, give them back what's theirs with a cherry on top. Pay your debt with honor.

Too few people walk that walk. To this day, I don't know if there really was a robbery in my associate's house. But because of that I let it go, like I've had to let go so many other bad loans.

I try not to lend money anymore. It became a very bad habit for me.

Give to Get

The funny thing about money is that the more you give, the more you get back, even if the cash doesn't always make a direct line back into your pocket.

Of course, it's not just about cash karma. It goes deeper than that. The right kind of giving and service can also reward you a hundred times over with the gift of personal fulfillment.

As soon as you've reached a point where you know you and yours will be taken care of, you have to stop focusing on the paycheck. The money will come if you work hard and think about other people. For those of us who've made it through the struggle that's not an option, it's an obligation.

It's important for our culture to give back. Anyone who has

made money in business has taken dollars from people who can't afford it. We weren't entitled to that success. We have to give back to our community. We have to say by our actions, "Hey, we appreciate you."

True success is not about getting paid, it's about paying it forward. We need to set a precedent for others, so that we can create our own tradition of philanthropy, hip-hop style. Whether we are businesspeople, rap artists or athletes, we have to be role models of giving so that when more kids come up from a life of poverty, the example has been set.

It's not just our responsibility to give back to the community, it's our privilege. Rich or poor, DO SOMETHING, whether it's just writing a check or giving up your time to teach and help others. You are never too good to serve.

I was lucky enough to have this ingrained in me from day one. I was raised by parents who not only made sacrifices for me, but for our community. You know, when your grandmother wasn't just *your* grandmother, but the whole neighborhood's grandma? When your father didn't just stop the ice cream truck to buy a frozen cup for you, but for all the kids on the block? That's where philanthropy starts.

You're never too young to develop a sense of service. The former president of VH1 has an eight-year-old daughter who goes to a New York City public school where some of her classmates are so poor they can't afford a new pair of shoes, let alone a decent pair. That young lady had a birthday coming up. But she told her parents she didn't want to have a party. Instead, she wanted to have a food drive.

Before I started my first year at Morgan State University, I went into the engineering summer program and met a kid my own age from outside D.C. who didn't have enough money for textbooks and had nowhere to live. Come fall semester, my parents took him in.

We had a finished basement, so he lived downstairs. We did our homework together, and I shared my textbooks with him. Occasionally, my parents would slip him money to help out with his expenses. There wasn't any question about it. The spirit of giving is so innate to my parents. To them, it's just something you do, like getting up in the morning and going to bed at night.

It didn't cost us much to do the right thing, but it made a huge difference in someone's life. My friend had the ability and will to help himself, but an unstable home and poverty were holding him back. He's in the military now, but every time he's back home he stops in and sees my parents.

That was just one of dozens of generous acts I witnessed in the home I grew up in. Charity really does begin at home. You watch how your own family treats others and it gets bred in the bone. My mother and father live by Martin Luther King's creed:

> Everybody can be great because anybody can serve. You don't have to have a college degree to serve. . . . You only need a heart full of grace, a soul generated by love . . .

Pay It Forward

I'm not trying to be holier than thou. Giving feels good. One of the most satisfying moments of my life was when I was able to help my old high school, Woodlawn, build a football stadium. In 2002 the school board needed $150,000 to get the project started, so I gave them a check.

Today, northwest Baltimore, one of the poorest sections of the country, has a facility to be proud of. What used to be a muddy field is now a state-of-the-art, multipurpose sports stadium with proper seating and a press box. Every time I pass by

I get a rush just knowing that members of my old high school football team can hold their heads up high.

Kids who felt diminished by the fact that they didn't have the same quality sports field as schools in richer suburbs can take pride in what they have now. Teenagers who might be hanging out in the street, up to no good, have a place to go to develop their potential and maybe even win sports scholarships.

It's important to give back to your own community and focus on the needs that you know exist. Checkbook charity is all well and good, but the money is better spent when you roll up your sleeves and figure out what's needed and where.

My friend Frank Ski, the Atlanta radio deejay, realized this at a recent Little League football game. Frank went to see his seven-year-old niece cheer at the game in a county just outside of Baltimore. By coincidence, an inner-city team he sponsors was playing that day.

When Frank's team stepped off the bus, wearing hand-me-down uniforms with their names written in magic marker and their shoes full of holes, the contrast with his niece, cute as a button with matching bows in her hair, made Frank feel like crud.

He went up to the coach and asked him why his team was looking so raggedy when he was sending those checks every month. The coach explained that it cost $50 just to register each kid on a Little League team. The rest of the money went to bus them back and forth to each game.

The experience inspired Frank to start a foundation that would track how every penny gets spent and get money to the overlooked community causes that need it most. He wants his organization to act as a go-between for the people with the money, like the NFL stars who don't know where their charitable donations are going, and the community organizations that need the most help.

In fact, NFL stars had come up through the team he was sponsoring, but none of them helped out because they had no clue how poor these kids were.

A few hip-hop entrepreneurs are following a similar path. More of us are creating a culture of giving through formal structures like charitable foundations. We want to manage our giving hands-on, to make sure we can have the greatest impact on the causes we care about.

Ludacris started the Ludacris Foundation in Atlanta to provide college scholarships and organize young kids to do volunteer work in their communities. I've just started the Kevin Liles for a Better Baltimore Foundation to provide funds for scholarships to Baltimore community colleges and Morgan State. I'm also funding college tours to black colleges and helping kids pay for youth sports and the Boy Scouts.

Russell Simmons started Rush Philanthropic to nurture arts and help artists in the urban community get exposure and access. He has given away millions of dollars in scholarships, and led the way in advocacy for prisoner rights and voter registration. He has paid out of his own pocket to hold a series of Hip-Hop Summits around the country to register thousands of young voters.

Russell is worth a lot of money. He could have put his feet up and retired. He could spend his days partying and hanging out at his houses in the Hamptons or the Caribbean with all the beautiful people. He has worked hard all his life, so he's entitled. But he says the most fun he's ever had in his career has been the building of Rush Philanthropic.

The other day, Russell told me about a group of kids who won a trip to New York to see him. "People were f_____ listening to me," he said. "Kids listening to what I say and coming back to me years later and telling me that it was because of me they went to college, that's one hell of a gift."

These days, the Godfather of Hip Hop cares more about giving than making money off the business empire he built. He says he'll die happy if it says "philanthropist" on his tombstone. His only regret is not discovering this joy earlier in his life.

Maybe it sounds a little grandiose to say that's how I want to be remembered too. There is a belief that true charity is anonymous and I don't disagree. But we also need to show and tell in this culture so that the next generation that comes up aspires to do the same.

I want my foundation to become a national, and maybe even an international, network of giving. Our culture has only just begun a tradition of giving. When those of us who know the struggle and the needs of our communities better than anyone finally get organized, think how powerful that will be.

Values, Pass Them On

Even if you don't practice giving for yourself, do it for your family.

One of the biggest challenges of success is making sure your own kids appreciate where it's come from and giving them the will to use their privileged position to make a difference in the world.

My daughter Kayla is only five, and Kevin Jr. just turned seven, but I remind them every day that there are others much less fortunate than them. I make sure they mix with people, whether they are poorer relatives or friends from school. I want my kids to see what the needs of the community are. I want to plant those seeds of compassion early on. When my kids grow up, I want them to oversee my own philanthropic foundation. I want them to have millions so that they can give away millions.

Just because you're wealthy doesn't mean your kids have to grow up spoiled rotten. They can have awareness beyond the value of a dollar. Take them to museums, show them the world and communicate with them every day. Give them the best education that money can buy, and that love and commitment can bestow.

I take a page out of LL Cool J's book. He doesn't want his kids to take anything for granted. So every night he makes his daughter write a short essay about great black women in history and he makes his son write a paper about great black men in history. It forces them both to look outside their own advantaged lives and aspire to be something great.

Foundation or no foundation, the values you pass on to your family will be your greatest legacy.

RULE 9

What: Don't Let Cash Rule

Why: Greed can trip you up. Money matters, but it's only a means to more options, freedom and security for the future.

How: Don't hoard, but don't spend money on diamonds and platinum as if it's your last day on earth either. Live well, but set aside some horizontal money. Property, bonds and stocks will generate wealth even while you're lying on your back!

But: Be generous. Giving back to your family and your community will have its own rewards.

Flex Purpose, Not Power

The leader's unending responsibility must be to remove

every detour, every barrier to ensure that vision is first

clear, then real . . .

—Jack Welch, former chairman and CEO of General Electric

Big ups! You've gotten this far and now you're on your way to the top of your game. Whether you're a sales assistant working toward floor manager, or a marketing director shooting for senior vice president, it's never too soon to learn how to lead.

Whatever you choose to do in life, the ability to take charge lies within you. It's up to you to decide if you're going to be a leader or a follower.

Leadership has nothing to do with job title. Some people were born with CEO written all over them. They're the stars of the business world. People instinctively follow a natural-born leader. Even when they're just interns making photocopies, they have an ability to inspire and lead by example.

Wherever you are on your come-up, aspire to lead, because it's one and the same with the desire to be the best you can be at whatever you are doing.

Great leaders aren't dictators who use their position to order around the people working under them. They don't flex power. They aren't rulers. They are enablers. They get their grind on and figure out the best way to inspire, instruct and motivate the team. They have the humility and wisdom to understand that leadership is synonymous with service.

I don't want to be the plug. I don't want to be the sole source of power. I want to be the outlet so that people can plug into me.

I've never thought of myself as the top dog. I'm whatever I need to be wherever I need to be to serve the people who work with me and help them do their jobs. I'm the facilitator, motivator, friend and police officer. It's not about me, it's about the team. I tell everybody what our goal is and let them go to it. If they ask for help, I give it to them. But if I've led well and surrounded myself with the best people, I know they'll get it done.

Over the years I've come to realize that employees work hardest if they clearly understand and embrace the mission. They follow the coach when he calls the play because they believe it will help them shine on the field, not because they are in awe or fear of the power you wield through your title and position.

They execute the plan not because you are telling them what to do, but because they see and believe in their own hearts what you are trying to accomplish. They want what you want, because they realize that they are working toward something that is bigger and greater than they are. They'll follow you anywhere to make it happen.

It's your responsibility not to abuse that power. If you are going to be a role model, make sure it's the right kind. Whether you are managing a record store or running a Fortune 500 company, power comes through empowering others to get things done.

Like Jack Welch, the legendary leader of GE, said, leadership is about "turning people loose to dream, dare and win."

Set the Example

When I first started at Def Jam's New York office, I watched everyone. I'd worked for a regular business before. World Connections Travel taught me a lot about managing a large group of people, but this was something new. This was a corporate culture in the making and the rules were only just being written.

The first thing that struck me was that the only person in that door before 9 a.m. was Lyor Cohen. Here was the president of the company, alone in the building, with no assistant to bring in the daily report of radio plays or go over his schedule, and no department heads checking in with him to discuss the meetings ahead before things went off the hook. It was crazy to me.

So I started coming in at 8:30. It wasn't easy. I was sleeping at my girlfriend's house while I was looking for a place, and the commute could take as long as two hours. I had no fixed address for months because I was always traveling. But to me it was only common sense that someone should get to the office before the boss did. Soon, embarrassed to see me sitting at my desk and personally answering all the calls, my assistant started coming in at 8:30 too.

Eventually the other assistants noticed the actions of my assistant, and they started trickling in before 9 a.m. Even today, Walter, the former intern, prides himself on beating me into the building every morning and having all of the daily reports arranged neatly on my desk.

There was a ripple effect throughout the entire floor just because one person set the example and another followed.

While other music executives at rival labels were sleeping it off after hitting the clubs the night before, we got more done during those early hours of the day. We were better prepared for our meetings and the whole organization started taking on a more professional sheen.

I watched Russell too. He had a way of making people want what he wanted for the company through raw passion and force of will. He wouldn't accept excuses. You couldn't say to him, "That's impossible." To Russell, impossible was nothing. How could you tell the man who'd built a thriving business empire out of a culture that was so overlooked it couldn't get a spin on the radio that it can't be done?

When I had just started at Def Jam in Baltimore, I listened in on a call with Russell on the line from New York. He was ripping into the team. We'd just had an "Impact Day," where we would try to convince all the radio stations to play a new record. There we were in the hottest hip-hop market in the country, yet somehow the spins just weren't happening. It was inexcusable. We were screwing up badly. Russell started firing people on the spot.

I was just an unpaid intern at the time, so I escaped his wrath, but that bawling out introduced me to another side of leadership. He was angry not because his team didn't get the play, but because we *could* have gotten the play and we just didn't deliver. The experience taught me that I never want to be in a position where I have to question whether or not someone goes above and beyond for me.

It also showed me that sometimes you do have to go there to wake people up and get the best out of them. You don't have to rule by fear, but there will be times when you have to bare your teeth to remind people that when they don't play their position, there are consequences.

Russell and Lyor each taught me that leadership is the ability to inspire a combination of respect and the desire to emulate among those who follow. Be an example, but back it up with strength.

Follow the Example

I've studied leaders throughout my whole career. Every time I see or read about business executives who are effective, I try to incorporate some of their leadership style and philosophy into my own brand of management. But I don't imitate. I assimilate.

You have to know who's out there. If you don't, go online or buy yourself a few issues of *BusinessWeek*, *Fortune* and *Forbes* and get educated. You don't have to apologize for not being aware of who the top executives are. But once you have been made aware, there is no excuse for staying uninformed.

I had my head down in my own industry for so long, I didn't even know who the big corporate players were. One day I was in a meeting with Lyor and he laughed at me and said, "You remind me of Dick Parsons."

I said, "Who you calling a dick?"

It's embarrassing to admit that, until recently, I didn't know who the CEO of Time Warner was. African-American Fortune 500 CEOs are so rare you can literally count them on one hand, but I was ignorant. I made it my business to find out.

I want to know everything about the men and women of all colors who defied the odds and broke into the highest ranks of corporate America. I want to know how they did it. I want to find out if there is something in their character, career path and leadership style that I can bring out in myself. I want to follow their example.

The truly great leaders all have very different qualities that make them successful. But they have one thing in common: they are quiet and unassuming. These executives don't need to shout. They don't have to have their faces splashed on the cover of *BusinessWeek* or *Fortune*. They're effective because of what they do and how they manage the people they work with. They are more liked than feared.

In Jim Collins' book *Good to Great*, he describes the kind of leader necessary to take a company to new heights of success:

> **Compared to high profile leaders with big personalities who make the headlines and become celebrities, the good-to-great leaders seem to have come from Mars. Self-effacing, quiet, reserved, even shy—these leaders are a paradoxical blend of personal humility and professional will.**

Kenneth Chenault, the CEO of American Express, is the perfect Martian. He's fiercely ambitious, but without all the rough edges that can make enemies along the way. He's a country boy with humble beginnings who came up when there was still segregation. Study him closely.

He's never been known to have lost his temper or raised his voice. He takes the trouble to chat to secretaries and ask them about themselves. He's mentored dozens of aspiring young managers. He keeps his door open and encourages people to step inside his office and say what's on their minds. His quiet confidence and human touch wins the respect of his employees and gets them to believe in the mission.

At the same time, he does what's necessary. In the mid-'90s, when the company's Travel Related Services division needed major reform, he eliminated 15,800 jobs and cut $3 billion in costs. He personally visited each of the nine centers where the cutbacks would be made and explained in detail to the staff exactly why the layoffs had to be.

Dick Parsons is another one of the great corporate leaders,

black or white, male or female. It's not surprising to me that he and Ken Chenault are good friends. Read up on him too.

Parsons came up from the mean streets of one of the poorest neighborhoods in Brooklyn in the '70s. He aced law school and became a top political advisor in Washington, D.C., where he worked with President Gerald Ford. Later on he switched careers from law to banking. Then he moved to Warner and got his corporate grind on.

By the time he was made chairman and CEO of Time Warner Inc. two years ago, the company was still flailing from the bad end of a bad deal with AOL and in desperate need of rescue. It had a loss of $54 billion and nearly $27 billion in mounting debt.

By 2004, the company was on its way to recovery, with a net profit of almost $2 billion and its debt reduced by almost half. It was no miracle. Parsons made it happen through common sense and hard work. He sold off the money-losing businesses and acquired new cable channels to build up healthy new profits.

By going back to the basics of what Time Warner does and moving on from the past, he's brought hope back to a demoralized workforce of 80,000 people worldwide.

People said it would take a Superman to turn around the world's biggest media company. But this guy is no flashy executive. People say it's his focus, his ability to analyze the facts and get to the bottom line and his ability to motivate an organization that make him successful as a leader. But these are not qualities that hit you over the head when you first meet the guy.

He's tall, bearded, quiet, unassuming and friendly. People like him, but he hates the limelight and would rather stay behind the scenes to get the work done. He can make the tough decisions and he can fire people, but he does it for the right reasons. He's the nice guy with the killer instinct and the desire to win.

Known as the "anti-mogul," he demonstrates that it's all

about keeping your head down and letting your work speak for you. "Keep a low profile," he's been quoted as saying. "It's an advantage to be underestimated. If you do your job well, you create the foundation of success."

It's executives like Dick Parsons, and my new boss, Edgar Bronfman Jr., who inspired me to expand my horizons and make my next move to Warner Music Group. My new position affords me the opportunity to apprentice with some of the greatest executives in the world. Together with my old mentor Lyor, I want to learn how to manage a billion-dollar business and understand where I fit in a larger media empire that does more than make records.

Working with the best in the business will help me take my game to the next level and beyond.

Walk the Floor

Once you find yourself in a position where you are in charge of others, whether it's a team of three or three hundred, make sure you are familiar with your people and what they do. Walk the floor, talk to them and let them see your face. One of my best qualifications for running a company is my MBWA—Management by Walking Around.

When I first started at Def Jam's New York offices, I used to go through the halls and yell, "Wooohooo, Wooohooo!" at the top of my voice. I'd stick Post-it Notes on every cubicle wall with inspirational, motivational messages. I know it sounds crazy, but I was trying to whip up the same level of excitement in my crew that I felt every day coming into the job.

After a while I had to stop. Our company got so big we had to spread out onto three floors, and I would have run out of breath before I'd walked and shouted down every hallway.

But every few days, I'd still make sure I walked over to the different departments and vibe with my people. Employees feel more comfortable when you meet them on their turf, and when people feel more comfortable, they will tell you stuff.

You'll get to know where their heads are at, and they'll feel you. People will always be more motivated when they have a greater appreciation for what you want and expect from them.

When I was coming up at Def Jam I worked various departments. I always had my territory covered, but when I was in promotions, I'd get involved in marketing and sales. When I was into branding I'd also have my finger in A&R. It helped me play my own position better to understand that I was just one piece of a larger puzzle.

You need the creative people to make the product that you're pushing and you need the sales people to get it into the record stores. You need the radio people to get it played on the radio and you need the video people to make the video that gets the artist on BET or MTV. You need the street teams pushing the vinyl on the college campuses and you need the managers to get the artists on the road to perform.

Dabbling in the different functions of the business made me more versatile and better equipped for a senior management role. But even if you haven't tried everyone else's hustle on your way up the ladder, you can gain the insight by talking to your best team players and making yourself accessible to them.

To gain the respect of your people, you have to be able to understand their language and know their jobs at least as well as they do. If I don't do my homework I leave myself open to hearing excuses.

People know that when they come in for a meeting with me, they'd better be prepared, because I'll detect the BS. A good coach has to know how all the positions are played. If I don't appreciate the particular challenges they face, I can't point them in the right direction.

Even when you can't walk the floor, leave the door to your office open as often as you can. Make it easy for your people to come to you. You don't want them to run to you for every little problem, but when something big goes down, you should be the first to know the problem and the solution.

The greatest benefit to leading through an open door is the environment you create. When people feel confident, they are more willing to take risks. That's a good thing.

When I took over from Lyor as president of Def Jam six years ago, he told me, "Kevin, remember, vulnerability is critical. If you can't risk yourself with your co-workers, you have a dysfunctional organization. No one will push the envelope and you'll lose out on the best ideas."

An atmosphere of fear creates divisiveness. People are so busy covering their own asses and playing politics that they stop thinking out of the box and trying to come up with original ideas. They're afraid they'll be shot down. It can spell the death of the entrepreneurial spirit.

Know Your Limits

I'll tell you straight up, I still have a lot to learn. Hell, I'm only thirty-seven years old. True wisdom takes time.

I've come very far, very fast, but in many ways I've reached the beginning of a whole new phase in my career.

I aspire to be one of the great leaders of Corporate America. It's always been my goal to break through some of the barriers to our culture and make it to the very top of a Fortune 500 company. But I'm working my way up from the bottom of a steep learning curve.

I've made my share of mistakes. Early on at Def Jam, I was a beast. Back then it was all about the winning. I'd do anything to turn no into yes. I wouldn't accept anything less than the best performance. If someone didn't deliver I'd tear him a new ass-hole.

Because I was single-minded and determined about bringing the label to the next level, I'd work eighteen-hour days and I would expect everyone around me to do the same. I couldn't understand how anyone else could want to live a life outside the building.

I didn't care what the problem was, who did what, or what the holiday was. None of that. I only cared about winning by any means necessary other than cheating. I didn't tolerate people who didn't display the same level of passion and obsession that I had.

It was so crazy that I couldn't even sit still in the hospital when my son Kevin Jr. was born. Six years ago, around the same time I was promoted to president of Def Jam, my child's birth was about the only event in my life that was big enough to pull me away from the office. But even that didn't keep me out of work mode for long!

I remember sitting in the maternity ward while my wife was in labor, talking away to the office on my Blackberry. The nurse gave me hell because you're not supposed to use cell phones in the hospital, so I switched it off, sat in the chair next to my wife's hospital bed, threw up my arms and said, "Okay, what do you want me to do now?"

Being cut off from my office, even when something that important was going on in my personal life, made me go all twitchy. A few hours later, when the baby was delivered, I was allowed to go see him in that viewing room with all the cribs.

A nurse was holding up a baby, so I yelled at her through the glass partition, "Is that my son? Lemme see my son!"

"No sir," she said. "This is a girl."

Finally, she brought out my baby boy to show me. I gave him a quick once-over and counted his ten fingers and ten toes. Satisfied that my son was fine and the wife was good, I told my homeboy Rod, who was with me at the time, "Okay, we good. There's nothing more for me to do. Let's get out of here."

In the car on my way back to the office for a meeting I didn't want to miss, I told Rod all about how my son was going to be in Little League baseball, Pee Wee football and the Boy Scouts.

Rod said, "Yo, Kevin, give the kid a break, he's only three hours old!"

But that was my mind-set back then. I couldn't grasp the concept of kicking back and appreciating life moment by moment. The idea of a work-and-life balance was alien to me. I was too switched on. My chronic sense of urgency wouldn't allow me to change gears.

I missed a lot of important events in my son's and daughter's early childhoods because I was always either at work or traveling for work. (That lifestyle cost me my marriage.) Until recently, I was getting three hours of sleep a night. I got myself so sick and run down a few years ago that I couldn't get out of bed for three days.

In many ways I still don't get how to balance the personal with the professional. When I socialize, it's with people in the industry. It's all shoptalk, all the time. I never do anything social without a purpose that somehow relates to the business.

I don't know what to do with myself during those short periods of downtime. Every time I have a spare few minutes, instead of sitting still, I'm checking the messages on my Blackberry or making calls. I don't sit back and chill in the car ride home. I'm either backseat-driving or running conference calls.

But as I've matured, I no longer expect everybody to be like me. I understand that some people are at 200 percent and others are at 75. Depending on the moment they're at in their life, the level of their intensity changes.

It doesn't necessarily hurt to have a life outside the building. In any consumer-based business, when you are living like a normal person you are also getting in touch with the needs and wants of the customer.

My expectations are still high, but they're more realistic. Nowadays, if somebody is going through something personal, I'll listen and give what I can to enable him to do his job. I'm more accepting of the fact that employees are human beings.

I'm also discovering that I can be just as effective even when I'm not working until eleven at night. I'm getting seven hours of sleep instead of five. I'm trying to take care of my health by squeezing in an hour with a personal trainer in between meetings.

It gets to a point where you have to show up for your life as well as for your job. If one of my kids has a school play, I'll leave the office a little earlier and work in the car on the way. Two years ago I started taking vacations for the first time in my life. I liked it so much that one week off became two. Now I go away twice a year.

To lead well, you have to get yourself straight. Like the saying goes, "He that would govern others, first should be the master of himself."

Leaders are as different as the businesses they're in. We have to change and adapt as the company we run evolves and grows. When Def Jam was building itself up from an entrepreneurial business with a staff of twenty, my hard-ass style was appropriate. During our grind years, they needed a micromanaging, workaholic maniac like me.

As Def Jam became a major player with more than two hundred employees, I had to learn to loosen my choke hold. I couldn't expect to be hands-on with that many people under me. I had to trust that my top managers were on it. I had to be smart enough to put the right people in the right positions, so that they could inspire their own teams and pass the message on down.

I can still be an asshole. Members of my team complain that I don't subscribe to Jack Welch's "kick and hug" theory. My management style is more "kick and kick." They know me as the big brother with the tough love. It's when I stop kicking that they worry, because they know it means I've given up on them.

Each merger and demerger, each expansion of the brand, has brought new lessons in leadership. I'm tweaking all the time as I learn to become more corporate while still retaining my entre-preneurial edge. I've stopped trying to do everyone else's job. I'm letting people free-fall. I've learned that you have to allow the people under you to make their own mistakes. It's how they learn.

I've also come to realize there are times when you need to shut the door. Leaders need to maintain an aerial view of what's going on. They need a break from all the noise. You can't step back and take in the whole if people are constantly in your ear or in front of your face.

I have to evolve from an executor to a planner. I need to take a break from putting out the fires so that I can reflect on what is happening and where I need to go next. I'm still working on that.

Be Mindful

If you've followed Rules 1 through 9, you already have the mak-ings of a successful career in business. You'll go as far as you want to in your chosen field. But ask yourself, "Do I really want to lead?" You have to decide if you want to carry that rock and take responsibility for the whole team.

If you choose this path, if you do decide to make CEO or president your ultimate goal, either through running your own business or rising within a corporation, make sure you under-stand the sacrifice involved. When you take that step, it's no less serious than becoming the head of a family. A very big and time-consuming family.

I have to be away from my own family all the time. I phone my kids every morning, but the hardest question I have to answer is from my son. "Daddy, why aren't you here?"

I say, "Daddy wants to be right there with you, but he's working hard. Why do you think that is?"

My son always knows the answer. "To pay for the car, the pool, the house. Because you're looking after us." Kevin Jr. understands, but I know he'd trade in a lot of the stuff he has to spend more time with his father. That's a tough one.

A lot of senior executives at Def Jam have chosen not to start a family because they fear they won't be able to spend enough time on their personal lives. It is what it is. No one forces you to choose that career path. Don't reap the rewards and then complain.

It's a great thing to be the boss. But it's a heavy load to carry, and many successful and respected executives ultimately decide not to take on the extra burden. Not everyone is cut out to be a great leader, and the decision to become responsible and accountable for an entire organization should never be an easy one.

Every day I am amazed by the impact my actions have on other people. If I walk into the office in a bad mood with a scowl on my face, it puts a cloud over the whole place. I am also aware of the power I have over an individual's desire to perform.

When I spin around in my desk chair and crank up the volume of a new artist's demo tape that I like, part of me is acting because I want the A&R person who delivered the tape to me to feel me. I want her to be as excited and motivated about what she is doing as I seem impressed with what she has brought me. I want her to say to herself, "Damn, he likes it! I must have done something right. I want that reaction from the boss more often."

I was reminded of how much my actions affect the people around me when I left Def Jam for the last time.

We had an intern named Nia. The niece of a senior executive at BET, she came on board a couple of months before I left. She's a bright young college graduate, but I hardly knew her. I just assumed she wanted to get into the music business.

A couple of days after I walked out of the building I got an e-mail. It was a long, thoughtful note from this young girl, telling me how disappointed she was that I had to leave Def Jam, because she'd taken the internship specifically so that she could work under me.

Here is what she wrote:

> Island Def Jam is not the brand, or at least not the current one. Kevin Liles is. I'm not sure if you remember the first time I had the opportunity of meeting with you and you mentioned you were interested in cultivating the youth of today into the leaders of tomorrow because Russell left you a legacy. I think that in the process you have created your own legacy. And I'm not saying this to be trite; I'm being real. As a member of the up and coming generation in the entertainment business, you are the leader I want to follow. I would choose to be on your team in any way I can.

That letter was a humbling reminder that it's not just about me. As a top executive I have the power to shape and influence the minds of tomorrow's leaders. That's no small consideration.

Handle Your Business

The first and greatest lesson I got in leadership will be my last to you. It came from my grandfather, Charles Bowie.

I'd always been close to my grandfather. My natural father

left while I was just a baby, so he became like a dad to me. Every chance I'd get I used to sit in his room, listen to the stories of his struggle and discuss the things I wanted to do in life.

Grandpa was a tall man. He stood at almost seven feet, or so it seemed to me. He and my grandma grew up dirt poor. He worked in a metal shop, but if he'd had the opportunity and access he would have become a doctor. His room was full of medical books. He was always reading up on science. Whenever he got hurt he could stitch himself up.

He was so tough that when he lost a finger in a factory accident, he calmly wrapped it up in a towel, walked home and threw it down on my grandmother's bed, his hand bleeding all over the place. That man was my rock!

When I was nineteen, me and the other guys in Numarx were on the road, on our way to Philadelphia to sign a contract with a new record label. But my mother called to tell me she thought my grandfather was having a heart attack. We'd only been half an hour on the road and I had to get home to see him, so we turned right back around to Baltimore.

When we got back to the clapboard semidetached house on Presstman Street, Grandpa was walking down the steps. He saw me coming up the path and said, "Boy, you know every now and then I get crazy."

I said, "Grandpa, you all right?"

He said, "Just come over here and give me a hug."

I gave him a hug and a kiss, then offered up my truck to take him to the hospital while I rode in the other car. He was so tall, I figured it would be easier for him to stretch out on the ride over.

Grandpa knew I had a big meeting to go to. I told him it didn't matter and that I would come with him to the hospital. But he saw my crew standing there. He knew they were counting on me to be there to make our big break happen. He wouldn't hear of me cancelling the meeting.

"Kevin, you go handle your business," he said.

Grandpa was always so strong, I figured he'd have to be all right. So we headed back up to Philly and had our meeting. After we signed the record contract, one of my band mates told me he got a call but he didn't want to tell me before the end of the negotiation. My grandfather had passed. He died before I could see him again. I was so depressed I couldn't work for days.

But I knew he was right. People were depending on me. Whatever personal loss I was going through, other people's dreams and livelihoods were at stake. My grandfather's last words taught me that the true meaning of leadership lies in personal sacrifice.

Now, go handle your business. Make it happen.

RULE 10

What: Flex Purpose, Not Power

Why: It's never too soon in your career to pick up a few management skills and learn how to lead.

How: Set the example. Don't ask someone to do something you wouldn't do yourself. Explain the mission and communicate to inspire and empower others. They will follow when they feel your passion for the cause.

But: Remember that leadership requires sacrifice. As you rise to the top you'll be giving up time with family and friends. Your life will not be your own when you are responsible for the livelihoods of other people.

THE TEN RULES, AGAIN

1. Find Your Will

Look deep inside to discover that thing you really love to do. You will need that passion to drive you to make it happen despite all the hard knocks along the way.

2. Do You

Discover your own flava, then package it and present it to the world. From the way you tie your shoelaces to how you get down to business, you are your own best brand.

3. Walk This Way

Get educated. Whether it's in college or the school of life, find a mentor, read and research. Knowledge will give you the tools you need to make it happen.

4. Create a Blueprint

Create a vision of what you want from life and draw a road map to success. Make planning and attention to detail part of the way you live your life.

5. Play Your Position

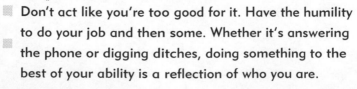

Don't act like you're too good for it. Have the humility to do your job and then some. Whether it's answering the phone or digging ditches, doing something to the best of your ability is a reflection of who you are.

6. Embrace the Struggle

Love the hard times because they make you stronger, wiser and more willing to take risks. Hard knocks breed tolerance and compassion. Failure teaches you how to do it better.

7. Get Connected

Build relationships to last forever. Success in business is built on personal networks. Kindness, tolerance and service will bring you repeat business.

8. Step Outside Your Box: M.I.X.

Be open to people from all walks of life. Reach out to those who are different from the usual crowd on your corner. Going global will help you blow it up even bigger.

9. Don't Let Cash Rule

Greed will only trip you up. Understand that money matters, but only as a means to freedom, access, options and security for the future. Learn how to make cash work for you.

10. Flex Purpose, Not Power

It's never too early to learn how to lead. Set the example. When you manage a team it's your job to inspire, motivate and empower your people.

A ROLE MODEL
FOR GENERATION HIP HOP

Kevin Liles was just another name on a long list of short profiles I had to produce for *Crain's New York Business*, the business weekly I write for. Every year, we publish a list of forty over-achieving New Yorkers under forty, and he was one of a crowd of successful young executives my editors decided to honor in 2003.

When I finally got an appointment with Kevin, after being rescheduled three times, I was mildly irritated and not predis-posed to being impressed. I had to catch this fish and write up the brief before I could go home for my Christmas vacation, and I figured I'd be lucky if I could get five minutes of his time. What was this insanely busy music executive going to tell me that I couldn't pull from his bio sheet anyway?

As I was ushered through Def Jam's glass and wood-paneled halls in midtown Manhattan to Kevin's corner office, I was also a little apprehensive. The latest rap hit was blaring on the office sound system as a dozen or so employees barely out of their teens darted between offices and worked the phones.

Knowing virtually nothing about hip hop other than what I'd read in the headlines about rap star shootings and drug convic-tions, I imagined meeting a cocky young man dripping in gold and diamond chains.

What I got instead was the polar opposite. Kevin's gentle manner put me immediately at ease. Slouched casually on his beige suede sofa wearing blue Phat Farm sweats, he could have been kicking back at his New Jersey mansion watching a foot-ball game. He had the street style typical of the hip-hop culture, but minus the flash I'd come to associate with a rap music mogul.

If anything, Kevin's combination of quiet diplomacy and workhorse business ethics reminded me of a Fortune 500 executive of an earlier generation. Here was a younger version of Time Warner Inc.'s chief executive Dick Parsons. Wise beyond his years, Kevin was just thirty by the time he was named president of the Def Jam label. He'd worked his way up from unpaid intern when he first joined the company nine years earlier.

Kevin has blended this straightlaced style with the high energy and creativity of his mentors: Def Jam's founder, Russell Simmons, and its former CEO, Lyor Cohen. In one unassuming package, he balances the entrepreneurial spirit of Def Jam's hip-hop roots with the sound, old-fashioned business sense needed to turn a member of this mercurial industry into a world-renowned entertainment empire.

I quizzed Kevin on all the usual stuff I needed to know for a seven-inch profile. Where was he from? Where did he go to school? What did he want to be when he was growing up in Baltimore? Surely the job of corporate executive wasn't at the top of his list?

Kevin had no pat answers. Instead, he paused to consider each question I tossed at him, replying with slow and thoughtful deliberation. Ignoring a barrage of incoming calls, he apologized for formulating his thoughts as he was speaking. His business style was so instinctive that he'd never thought to put into words what already came so naturally.

It was his first in-depth interview with the business media and he wanted to take the time to get his message across. He was eager to break the stereotype and deliver his truth about a consumer brand empire that has defined the taste of a generation and captured a youth market coveted by the mainstream business establishment.

Despite an international CD sales slump, cutthroat competition and a belief among many that the music of hip hop has had its day, Kevin helped transform Def Jam from a small but phenomenally successful record label with revenues of $30 million to a mature, $400-million-a-year corporation. Under his leadership, Def Jam Records quadrupled sales in four years.

Through partnerships with Russell Simmons' Rush Communications, Kevin was also instrumental in turning the Def Jam brand into a consumer and entertainment empire beyond music sales, building new businesses in clothing, video games, movies and mobile phone technology.

Still, I was skeptical. Companies don't grow that fast without some chaos. At best, his employees must be struggling with growing workloads, political backbiting and dramatic changes in the internal structure of the business. You don't expand and partner with corporate giants like Universal Music Group without leaving a few bodies behind. Why should Def Jam be any different?

"We are the brand of the people," Kevin explained. "Def Jam is one and the same with our culture, and we have a responsibility to the people we represent," he continued. "We *are* hip hop."

Somehow, he was able to craft a management style out of the very roots of hip hop and build a community within a company. He created a workforce that shares a creed.

Three decades ago, anyone with raw talent could be master of the mic at the block parties in Queens and the Bronx where the first rap artists entertained. The same egalitarian principles applied at Def Jam, where "it doesn't matter who you know or where you went to school. No one cares if you are poor, black, brown or white," Kevin said. "As long as you work hard and deliver, you can be a part of this team."

Most of Def Jam's team of two hundred workers was putting in at least twelve hours a day, because Kevin put in fifteen. Making no distinction between his business and his personal life, he brought the same tough but unconditional love to running Def Jam as he does to raising his own family.

"You give them a chance, you give them your trust, you include them and you tell them the truth," he said.

Kevin's way was to reward his hardest workers with more responsibility, instilling a sense of ownership in Def Jam and all it stood for. While a fan of Jack Welch and his groundbreaking leadership style at General Electric, "There's the GE Way and there's the Def Jam Way," he explained. "Def Jam stands for generation empowerment."

Beyond selling CDs, fashion and video games, creating this kind of working environment has opened the door to people who might not otherwise have had access to jobs in the business world. As a kid from West Baltimore, a neighborhood where he witnessed a street slaying at the age of nine, Kevin sees himself in the young fans of hip-hop music. He's made it his personal mission to open up their worlds and provide them with access and opportunity.

"I'm laying the blueprint so that kids from our culture know they have another option," he told me. "I believe I have a calling from God to help them change their lives and inspire them to be more. They can do that through business."

Kevin's not just referring to the music business. It was his ultimate goal to see many of the young executives brought up through the ranks of Def Jam move on to other types of industries. Kevin could see himself in an executive position at a Fortune 500 company like PepsiCo or American Express.

He'd happily switch industries if only to pave the way for others from his background. With his experience running a multimillion-dollar business, why shouldn't that be one of his options in the future, he asked.

"It should be," I thought to myself. "He could teach Jack Welch a thing or two."

It was early December 2002, when the business world was still roiling from the Enron scandal. Martha Stewart had just been accused of insider trading. Tyco was in trouble and Arthur Andersen was imploding. A string of revelations about dirty dealings on Wall Street had begun to surface.

Jobs were being slashed and life savings and pensions were being plundered by corporate bigwigs across America. As a New York City–based business reporter who has covered story after story of greed and corruption, I was struck by Kevin's back-to-basics wisdom.

Kevin had fostered a fierce loyalty that most businesses can only dream of at a time of profound disillusionment with corporate America. The president's door was open, literally. Even an eighteen-year-old intern from the mailroom felt comfortable enough to come in and ask him a question, one of many interruptions Kevin patiently bore during our conversation.

Two hours later, on my wintry walk back to the newsroom, I kept thinking about Kevin's fresh approach to leadership. Beautiful in their simplicity, his principles for success were founded on notions of integrity that should govern any workplace: inclusiveness, honesty and accountability.

In the two years since our first meeting, much has changed. Kevin is no longer president of Def Jam. Like so many other record companies, the pioneering label has undergone a tumultuous period. Early in 2004, Kevin's own boss and mentor, Lyor Cohen, moved on to become CEO of Warner Music Group. Kevin also resigned. But, recognizing that he was the life and soul of the brand, executives at Universal begged him to stay.

Kevin withdrew his resignation a week later, trying in good faith to work with the new CEO, Antonio "L.A." Reid, a colleague in the music industry whom he'd long admired.

But it soon became clear that the record label was too small for both men. Kevin's loyal following among staff members created tension. He left "to maintain unity," he told me. "Divisiveness was making it impossible to have disciplined thought and disciplined action."

The stakes were too high and the relationships were too important to risk staying. "Def Jam was too great a brand, and L.A. was too good a friend, to allow the situation to continue," he explained.

As soon as word got out about Kevin's departure, the offers poured in. Fortune 500 companies, including American Express, were among those interested in snapping up the marketing and branding prodigy. Kevin could have had his wish to make waves outside the music industry sooner than he'd planned.

Instead, he decided to reunite with Mr. Cohen at Warner, a billion-dollar music business that's striving for more urban content. His position as the number two there makes him the highest-ranking and youngest African-American executive in the music industry. Operating within such a large media empire and watching the likes of Edgar Bronfman Jr. up close will give Kevin the opportunity to broaden his experience.

"I want to take my game to the next level and this is where I can continue to learn," he said. "I want to open more doors."

Through it all, Kevin practiced what he preached. He never uttered a word against Mr. Reid or Def Jam. Instead, he focused on building the brand and mentoring his staff, leaving the legacy in good shape and able to withstand the flood of changes to come.

"I didn't take them fishing, I taught them how to fish," he said. "They'll be fine without me."

—*Samantha Marshall*

MUST READ

Autobiography of Malcom X Introduction by Alex Haley (Random House)

Emile By Jean Jacques Rousseau, Edited by P.D. Jimack (Charles B. Tuttle Co.)

Good to Great By Jim Collins (HarperCollins)

Grinding It Out: The Making of McDonald's By Ray Kroc and Robert Anderson (St. Martin's Press)

Jack: Straight From the Gut By Jack Welch, John A. Byrne and Mike Barnicle (Warner Books)

Long Walk to Freedom By Nelson Mandela (Little, Brown)

48 Laws of Power By Robert Greene and Joost Elffers (Penguin)

Rich Dad, Poor Dad: What the Rich Teach Their Kids About Money That the Poor and the Middle Class Do Not! By Robert T. Kiyosaki and Sharon L. Lechter (Warner Books)

Roots: The Saga of an American Family By Alex Haley (Dell)

Sam Walton: Made in America By Sam Walton and John Huey (Bantam Doubleday Dell)

The Purpose-Driven Life: What on Earth Am I Here For? By Rick Warren (Zondervan)

The Tipping Point: How Little Things Can Make a Big Difference By Malcolm Gladwell (Little, Brown)

The 22 Immutable Laws of Marketing By Al Ries and Jack Trout (HarperCollins)

Who Moved My Cheese? An Amazing Way to Deal With Change in Your Work and in Your Life By Spencer Johnson (Putnam)

MUST HEAR

"Best Of Both Worlds" Jay-Z and R. Kelly on *The Best of Both Worlds*

"Can't Knock the Hustle" Jay-Z on *Reasonable Doubt*

"Drop It Like It's Hot" Snoop Dogg on *R&G (Rhythm & Gangsta): The Masterpiece*

"Fight the Power" Public Enemy on *Fear of a Black Planet*

"Hail Mary" 2Pac on *Greatest Hits*

"I Believe I Can Fly" R. Kelly on *R.*

"It's All About the Benjamins" P. Diddy and the Family on *No Way Out*

"Jesus Is Love" The Commodores on *Love Songs*

"Keep Ya Head Up" 2Pac on *Strictly For My N____z*

"Kick in the Door" Notorious B.I.G. (Biggie Smalls) on *Life After Death*

"King of Rock" Run DMC on *King of Rock*

"Lose Yourself" Eminem on *8 Mile* sound track

"Love" Musiq on *Aijuswanaseing*

"Momma Said Knock You Out" LL Cool J on *Momma Said Knock You Out*

"Please Listen to My Demo" EPMD on *Unfinished Business*

"U Don't Know" Jay Z on *The Blueprint*

"Warning" Notorious B.I.G. (Biggie Smalls) on *Ready to Die*

"We Gonna Make It" Jadakiss on *Kiss tha Game Goodbye*

"Who We Be" DMX on *The Great Depression*

MUST SEE

Pay It Forward, Scarface, Godfather I, II, III
Boyz N the Hood, Krush Groove, New Jack City, Forrest Gump,
Saving Private Ryan, Juice, Cooley High